Lincoln Christian College

P9-DFC-526

RICHELIEU

RICHELIEU

BY

RICHARD LODGE, M.A.

KENNIKAT PRESS
Port Washington, N. Y./London

RICHELIEU

First published in 1896
Reissued in 1970 by Kennikat Press
Library of Congress Catalog Card No: 77-112812
ISBN 0-8046-1079-7

Manufactured by Taylor Publishing Company   Dallas, Texas

CONTENTS

INTRODUCTION

CHAPTER I

RICHELIEU'S EARLY LIFE

1585-1614

43814

CHAPTER II

THE STATES-GENERAL—RICHELIEU'S FIRST MINISTRY

1614-1617

CHAPTER III

RICHELIEU AND THE QUEEN-MOTHER

1617-1624

CHAPTER IV

THE VALTELLINE AND LA ROCHELLE

1624-1628

CHAPTER V

CHAPTER VI

CHAPTER VII

REVERSES AND TRIUMPHS

1635-1640

CHAPTER VIII

DOMESTIC GOVERNMENT

CHAPTER IX

RICHELIEU AND THE CHURCH

CHAPTER X

RICHELIEU'S LAST YEARS

1641, 1642

INTRODUCTION

THE history of France from the tenth to the close of
the eighteenth century is bound up with the history of
the French monarchy.   Under the early Capets France
was a mere geographical expression ; its kings were
little more than the titular chiefs among a number of
feudal nobles, and their practical authority was limited
to the Ile de France.   From this powerless condition
the monarchy was gradually raised by the energy of
Louis VI., the prudence of Philip Augustus, and the
legislative ability and high personal character of Louis
IX.   But the real founder of absolute monarchy in
France was Philip IV., who created that administrative
system which gradually extended itself over the whole
kingdom, and undermined the independent local institutions of feudalism.   Successful war and the extinction

of the old mediæval families enabled the crown to bring most of the provinces under its direct rule. But a new danger arose from the practice of granting these provinces out as appanages to members of the royal family, who formed a new nobility as eager for independence as the feudal magnates whose place they had taken. At the same time the disasters of the wars with Edward III. and Henry V. seriously weakened the monarchy, which sunk again into impotence under John II. and Charles VI. But the falling structure was successfully rebuilt under Charles VII. and Louis XI. In the former reign the English were expelled, a standing army established, and a revenue secured by the imposition of the permanent *taille*. Louis XI. broke up the formidable League of the Public Weal, and the decline of the great Burgundian power on the death of Charles the Bold freed the French crown from its most dangerous rival. The marriage of the heiress of Brittany to two successive kings extinguished the independence of the last of the feudal provinces. The victory of the monarchy seemed to be assured, when Francis I., at the head of a compact and well-organised kingdom, successfully resisted the enormous but ill-compacted power of Charles V.

But a subtle evil was already undermining the foundations of this imposing edifice, and was destined in the end to overthrow it. This was financial maladministration. The chronic deficit, which was the chief immediate cause of the Revolution of 1789, was already in existence in the sixteenth century. It is not a little curious that France, the home of financial theories, has only produced in its long history three great financial administrators — Jacques Cœur, Sully, and Colbert; and their efforts only succeeded in postponing the inevitable crash. Among the ruinous expedients to which the crown was impelled by an empty treasury, the most fatal was the sale of offices. This practice, which originated in the fifteenth century, was raised into a system by Louis XII., who is said to have copied the usages of the Roman court. In order to make these offices valuable their holders must be irremovable. Thus the crown, of its own accord, surrendered the control over its own officials. The administrative institutions, such as the parliament of Paris, which had been the most efficient agents in extending the royal power, became in the seventeenth century the most serious opponents of royalty.

The period following the death of Henry II. (1560) is the most critical in the history of France. A country on which geography had imposed the necessity of unity, and which had risen to greatness in Europe by attaining that unity under a strong monarchy, was suddenly divided by the most powerful of forces—religion. Not only was the practical authority of the crown almost annihilated during the long struggle between Catholics and Huguenots, but its theoretical foundations were torn up and examined by polemical writers on both sides. While the Huguenots endeavoured to conciliate support by vindicating the independence of nobles and municipalities, the Jesuits taught that the voice of the people was the voice of God, and that circumstances might arise in which tyrannicide was not only a right but a duty. At the same time military necessities forced the kings to intrust the government of the great provinces to powerful nobles, who used their delegated authority in their own interests, and threatened to revive a military feudalism which recalled the anarchy of the twelfth and thirteenth centuries.

The struggle ended at last in the defeat of both the extreme parties ; and their defeat was due to their collision with that passionate desire for unity which has been the dominant force in French history from that day to this. The Huguenots, the prototypes of the later Girondins, aimed at establishing a system of local isolation, which must have effaced France from among the great states of Europe. The success of the League would have subjected the Gallican Church to Rome, and would have made France a vassal and tool of the Spanish Hapsburgs. The victory of Henry IV. and the middle party, which represented national interests and instincts, was secured by Henry's acceptance of Roman Catholicism, and by his grant of the Edict of Nantes to the Huguenots.

Henry IV. is a great as well as an attractive figure in history, and he deserves much of the idolatry with which the French have always regarded him. He restored order after the chaos of the religious wars. He founded the Bourbon monarchy, which was to preside for the next two centuries over the history of France, and was to guide that country to an ascendency in Europe, to which it still looks back with boastful regret. With the aid of Sully he restored the balance between income and expenditure, and encouraged the development of the internal resources of France. He humbled the power of Philip II., and inaugurated the foreign policy which was followed with such success by Richelieu, Mazarin, and Louis XIV.

But the work of Henry IV. was still incomplete, when he was removed by the dagger of Ravaillac. Neither he nor Sully had the genius or the foresight to found a new system of government, which was necessary for the triumph of the new dynasty. Even in the task of destroying abuses, both king and minister were trammelled by their past lives, and by the circumstances under which Henry had come to the throne. In some matters a policy of compromise was all that was possible for them. Under their rule the forces of disorder were checked rather than annihilated. Again, the provincial governorships remained in the hands of the great nobles, though their authority was limited by the appointment of lieutenant-generals, who were to act as the agents of the crown, and by the policy of intrusting the chief towns in a province to persons independent of the governor. And the supplementary clauses of the Edict of Nantes conferred upon the Huguenots, not only religious toleration, but also a political independence which enabled them to stir up disorder whenever it suited their interests. Above all, the sale of offices, instead of being abolished, was systematised by the institution of the *paulette*. Members of the parliament and of the other central courts, by paying an annual tax to the crown, became the absolute proprietors of their offices, which they could transmit to their heirs or dispose of by sale to whom they pleased. Thus the office-holders in France came to form a vast hereditary corporation, with corporate interests to defend, and virtually independent of the crown. The nobles, the Huguenots, and the sovereign courts, were left by Henry IV. to be the great obstacles in the way of his successors.

The insecurity of the monarchy under these conditions was clearly manifested during the regency of Mary de Medici. There are few more depressing and wearisome periods of history than the first thirteen years of the reign of Louis XIII. The incessant intrigues of the great princes against the crown and against each other, the complete subordination of national to personal interests, the petty rivalries of the Huguenot leaders, Bouillon and Rohan, the coalitions against the queen's favourite, Concini, and against the king's favourite, Luynes, have been described in contemporary memoirs with a fulness which they only merit as an effective contrast to the state of things which preceded and which followed them. The regent and her ministers purchased a few years' peace by lavish bribes to the nobles at the expense of the monarchy, while she sought to strengthen herself against domestic opposition by abandoning the foreign policy of her husband, and concluding a close alliance with Spain. The revival of the Hapsburg supremacy, threatened in the first period of the Thirty Years' War, was allowed to progress without hindrance from France.

From these disorders and dangers France was saved by the greatest political genius she has ever produced. No man was ever more completely a politician than Richelieu, and no figure is more indispensable in a series which professes to form a gallery of " Foreign Statesmen." His own memoirs treat of nothing but politics. The character of the man himself must be looked for in the accounts of contemporaries, few of whom were able to estimate his greatness or to appreciate his aims. The details of his private life have to be gleaned from scattered sources, but chiefly from the letters and papers which have been edited in so masterly a manner by M. d'Avenel.

In writing the life of Richelieu one must narrate the history of France and, to a great extent, of Europe during an eventful period of nearly twenty years. Perhaps this consideration helps to explain why no first-rate biography of him has been produced, even in France. In spite of the innumerable books that have been written on this period, the work of Aubéry, although an avowed panegyric, and published as long ago as 1661, has never been completely superseded. It is to be hoped that M. Hanotaux may yet find sufficient leisure amid the distractions of political life to continue the great work which he has begun, and that this will fill what is an undoubted *lacuna* in historical literature. In the meantime this little volume can only attempt a brief estimate of the work which Richelieu achieved—and achieved with such success that he must be regarded as the chief founder, not only of France before the Revolution, but of much that is most characteristic of France at the present day.

CHAPTER I

1585–1614

The family of du Plessis—The du Plessis de Richelieu—Career
of François du Plessis—Birth of Armand Jean—His life at
Richelieu—He enters the College of Navarre—Transferred to
the Academy—The bishopric of Luçon—Armand returns to the
University—Consecrated bishop at Rome—He quits Paris for
Luçon—Motives for this step—Letters to Madame de Bourges
—His conduct as bishop—His religious attitude—Early relations with Jansenism—Connection with Bérulle and Father
Joseph—Death of Henry IV.—Richelieu in Paris—Acquaintance with Barbin and Concini—Returns to his diocese—His
attitude towards parties at court—Letter to Concini—Election
to the States-General—Personal appearance—Feeble health—
Character and aims.

THE family of du Plessis has no history. For generations it had lived in provincial obscurity on the borders
of Poitou. In the fifteenth century François du Plessis,
a younger member of the family, inherited the estate of
Richelieu from his maternal uncle, Louis de Clérembault.
His descendants were the du Plessis de Richelieu, and
their chief residence was the castle of that name, situated
on the Mable, near the frontier of Poitou and Touraine.

The first member of the family who played any notable part in history was François du Plessis, great-

grandson of the inheritor of Richelieu. He rendered valuable services to Henry of Anjou during his brief tenure of the crown of Poland, and retained his favour when he returned to France as Henry III. Raised to the dignity of grand provost of France, François du Plessis became one of the most prominent and loyal servants of the last of the Valois. When his master died under the dagger of Jacques Clément, it was he who arrested the assassin and took down the depositions of the eye-witnesses.

The death of Henry III. left his Catholic followers in a difficult position. The traditions of his family seemed to impel François du Plessis to join the League. But he showed on this occasion a practical foresight worthy of his great son, and at once espoused the cause of Henry of Navarre. He had already gained the confidence of the new king by his bravery at Arques and at Ivry, and had just been appointed captain of the guard, when he was carried off by a fever during the siege of Paris on July 10, 1590.

François du Plessis was married to Suzanne de la Porte, daughter of the celebrated *avocat*, François de la Porte, and herself possessed of the practical ability which characterised her family. They had three sons and two daughters, and the youngest child, Armand Jean, was born at Paris in the rue du Boulay, on September 9, 1585. The child was so feeble and sickly that it was not thought safe to have him baptized till May 5, 1586. His god-parents were Marshal Biron, Marshal d'Aumont, and his paternal grandmother, Françoise de la Roche-chouart.

Armand Jean was only five years old when his father

died, and his mother carried her children from the capital to the seclusion of Richelieu. There, amid the disturbances of the civil war between Henry IV. and the League, the boy's education was carried on for the next seven years. We have no evidence that he showed any youthful precocity or gave any signs of future greatness. Aubéry, who wrote under the auspices of Richelieu's relatives, and who would certainly have preserved any family traditions about his hero, tells us nothing of this period of his life, so that we may conclude that there was nothing to tell.

A distant province like Poitou offered few educational advantages in the sixteenth century, and at the age of twelve Armand was sent to Paris, and was admitted to the College of Navarre. There he went through the ordinary courses of grammar and philosophy, and an anecdote of his later years proves that he retained a grateful recollection of this period of his education. In 1597 Jean Yon, one of the philosophical teachers of the College of Navarre, held for the third time the office of Rector of the University, and the young scholar, robed as a chorister, accompanied him on a solemn procession to the tomb of St. Denis. In later days, whenever the University wished to prefer a petition to the all-powerful cardinal, the venerable Yon was always included in the deputation. Richelieu confessed that he never saw his old teacher without a sentiment of respectful fear, and the deputation, even if its request were not granted, was certain of a gracious answer from the minister.

At this time Richelieu was destined for a military career, and he had only received the usual rudimentary education when he was transferred from the College of

Navarre to the *Académie*, an institution founded by Antoine de Pluvinel to train the sons of noble families in the exercises and accomplishments which were to fit them for a soldier's life. It was here that Armand acquired the military tastes which never deserted him. He was at all times ready to exchange his cassock for a knight's armour, and equally willing to give his advice as to the handling of an army or the construction of a fortress.

The young marquis de Chillon, as he called himself at the Academy, was only seventeen years old when an event occurred which suddenly altered all his aspirations. In 1584 Henry III., in accordance with a practice not uncommon in those days, had granted to François du Plessis the disposal of the bishopric of Luçon. His widow, left in somewhat straitened circumstances, had found the revenues of the bishopric one of her chief resources. The episcopal functions were exercised in the meantime by one François Yver, who was avowedly only a " warming-pan " until one of the sons could take his place. But the chapter of the diocese resented the diversion of the episcopal revenue to secular and personal uses, and threatened to go to law with M. Yver, whose position was indefensible. In these circumstances Madame de Richelieu determined to procure the appointment of her second son, Alphonse Louis, to the bishopric. From 1595 he is occasionally spoken of as bishop of Luçon, though he never really held the office. Suddenly, about 1602, he absolutely refused to seek consecration, became a monk, and entered the Grande Chartreuse. In the next year M. Yver, on the suit of the chapter, was ordered by the parliament to devote a third of the

revenue of the bishopric to the repairs of the cathedral
and of the episcopal palace.

These events were a great blow to Madame de
Richelieu, but she had still one expedient left. By a
petition she delayed the enforcement of the decree of
parliament, and in the meantime her third son was to
assume the position which his brother refused. Armand
seems to have made no opposition to his mother's will.
In 1603 he quitted the Academy, and resumed his
studies at the University. His eldest brother, Henri,
was now at court, where Henry IV. had received him
with favour as his father's son, and where he was able
to defend the interests of his family. In 1606 the king
wrote to the French envoy at Rome, urging him to
obtain from the pope the appointment of Armand Jean
du Plessis to the bishopric of Luçon, although he had
not yet reached the canonical age.

Meanwhile Richelieu, who had taken deacon's orders
and completed his theological course in this year, became
impatient of the delays of the papal court, and hurried
to Rome to look after his own interests. He succeeded
in obtaining favour with the pope, and was consecrated
by the cardinal de Givry on April 17, 1607. There is
no foundation whatever for the story told in later years
by Richelieu's detractors that he deceived the pope as
to his age by producing a false certificate of birth, and
that when he afterwards confessed the fraud Paul V.
declared that "that young man will be a great rogue."
Equally unfounded is the counterbalancing story that
the pope was so impressed with Richelieu's stores of
theological learning that he exclaimed, *Æquum est ut
qui supra ætatem sapis infra ætatem ordineris* (It is only

fair that one whose knowledge is above his age should be
ordained under age).

On his return he resumed his studies at the University until, on October 24, 1607, he was admitted a
member of the Sorbonne or theological faculty. For the
next year he remained in Paris, acquiring a certain
reputation as a preacher, cultivating the acquaintance of
all who might be of use to him, and retaining the favour
of the king, who frequently spoke of him as "my bishop."
From the first, his ambition was for political distinction;
his avowed model was the cardinal du Perron, who had
acquired a great but fleeting reputation as the champion of
the orthodox creed against the Huguenots. Everything
seemed to attract the young prelate to remain in Paris :
in days when ecclesiastical duties sat lightly on church dignitaries, it appeared preposterous to expect him to reside
in a petty, unattractive provincial town like Luçon, far
removed from the capital, without society, with dull and
depressing surroundings, and close to the chief stronghold of the heretics.   Yet in 1608 Richelieu suddenly
determined to bury himself for a time in what he himself termed "the most villainous, filthy, and disagree-
able diocese in the world."

His motives for this step are wrapped in complete
obscurity.   It is certain that Henry IV., though no
strict champion of discipline, approved of prelates resid-
ing in their sees.   He may have hinted to the young
bishop that his newly-acquired position carried some
duties with it.   But it is more probable that the decision
was due to Richelieu himself.   He was always keenly
alive to practical considerations.   He may well have
felt that to obtain distinction he must do something to

deserve it. His powers were immature, and he had no
experience in the conduct of affairs. The bishopric of
Luçon was not a great stage to appear on, but it offered
opportunities for practical work, and its very neighbour-
hood to La Rochelle made it the more important at a
time when the position of the Huguenots might at any
moment become the most pressing question of the day.
It is possible that poverty may have been another
motive. The family estates were fairly extensive, but
they brought in a small revenue, and Richelieu was the
youngest child. Even his elder brother, who enjoyed
a considerable pension from the king, was always com-
plaining of want of funds. Richelieu was throughout
his life extremely sensitive to public opinion. He could
make a respectable figure as a resident bishop on an
income which was lamentably meagre for an aspiring
politician in Paris.

His first care was to provide himself with a residence.
His palace was in ruins, and in those days furnishing
was a matter of great expense and difficulty. His
letters to Madame de Bourges, who acted as a sort of
maternal adviser and purchaser for him in Paris, are
among the most interesting specimens of his correspondence, and illustrate that careful attention to details
which always characterised him. The following was
written in the spring of 1609, when he had already
been some months at Luçon.

"I shall not want for occupation here, I can assure you,
for everything is so completely in ruins that it needs much
exertion to restore them. I am extremely ill lodged, for
I have no place where I can make a fire on account of
the smoke. You can imagine that I don't desire bitter

weather, but there is no remedy but patience. . . .
There is no place to walk about in, no garden or alley
of any sort, so that my house is my prison.   I quit this
subject to tell you that we have not found in the parcel
a tunic and dalmatic of white taffety, which belonged to
the ornaments of white damask which you have pro-
cured for me : this makes me think that they must have
been forgotten. . . . I must tell you that I have bought
the bed with velvet hangings from Madame de Marcon-
net, which I am having done up, so that it will be
worth 500 francs.   I am also getting several other
pieces of furniture, but I shall want a tapestry. If it were
possible to exchange the valance of silk and gold from the
bed of the late bishop of Luçon for a Bergamasque
canopy, like that which you have already bought me,
it would suit me very well.   There are still at Richelieu
several portions of the said bed, such as the laths of the
framework, etc., which I could send to you.   You see
that I write to you about my establishment, which is
not yet well supplied : but time will do everything.   I
have secured a *maître d'hôtel* who serves me very well,
and in a way that would please you : without him I was
very badly off, but now I have nothing to do but to
look after my accounts, for whatever visitors come to
see me, he knows exactly what to do.   He is the young
la Brosse, who was formerly in the service of M. de
Montpensier."

In another letter of slightly later date he shows a
desire to impress his guests by his magnificence : " Please
let me know what would be the cost of two dozen
silver plates of the best size that are made.   I should
like to have them, if possible, for 10,000 crowns, for

my funds are not large ; but I know that for a matter of another hundred crowns you would not let me have anything paltry. I am a beggar, as you know, so that I cannot play the wealthy prelate ; but still, if I only had silver plates, my nobility would be much enhanced."

But Richelieu was not only occupied with the splendour of his table and the hangings of his bed. That he was, by the standard of those days, an excellent bishop, there can be no doubt. In his diocese he first found an opportunity to display those administrative talents which he was afterwards to employ in the service of his country. His correspondence shows that he took the widest view of his episcopal functions. Not content with admonishing his clergy, and seeking energetic recruits from all quarters, he also attended to the secular interests of his flock. In the hope of obtaining relief for their financial necessities, he writes urgent letters to the assessors of taxes, and even to the great duke of Sully. To his delight his merits begin to be appreciated. He hears that the cardinal du Perron speaks of him as a model for other bishops to copy.

Of Richelieu's attitude towards religion it is not easy to speak with precision. It was never the guiding force of his life ; at all times he subordinated religious interests to considerations of policy. No doubt has ever been cast upon the sincerity of his belief. Scepticism was in those days the luxury of a few leisurely and self-indulgent critics. Richelieu's essentially practical mind was averse to the speculative subtleties which lead to unbelief. Numerous passages in his memoirs show that he was more inclined to accept the current superstitions

of his time than too curiously to inspect the evidence
for them.

Still more difficult is it to lay down any formula
about his relations with ecclesiastical parties. At the
beginning of his career the chief divisions in France were
the Ultramontanes, the Gallicans, and the Huguenots.
To these were added before his death the Jansenists, a
sort of advanced guard of Gallicanism. To the Huguenots
Richelieu had no leaning, and he was ever ready to
enter the lists of controversy against them ; but he was
always personally tolerant towards them, both as bishop
and as minister. In a letter of 1611 he speaks of
Chamier, one of their most vehement and outspoken
champions, in terms of studied moderation : " He deserves
to be esteemed as one of the most amiable of those who are
imbued with these new errors, and if he may be blamed
for anything besides his creed, it seems to be a certain
too ardent zeal, which others might perhaps term indiscreet." With the sects of his own Church Richelieu's
relations changed at different periods, and each had at
times occasion to charge him with treachery or desertion.
So far as their differences were doctrinal rather than
political, he had no particular bias. He was a sufficient
master of the scholastic theology for controversial
purposes, as was proved by the works published during
his lifetime. But the real object of these writings was
to further his own advancement rather than to secure
the acceptance of his particular views. He had none
of the self-sacrificing enthusiasm and none of the
deeply-rooted conviction of the religious prophet or
martyr.

At one time there can be no doubt that he was

powerfully impelled towards Gallican, if not Jansenist, opinions. One of the neighbours of whom he saw most was Chasteignier de la Rochepozay, the fighting bishop of Poitiers, whose father had been the friend and companion-in-arms of François du Plessis. The bishop of Poitiers had appointed as his grand-vicar, Duvergier de Hauranne, afterwards abbé of St. Cyran, and famous as the apostle of Jansenism in France. Another link in the chain was Sebastien Bouthillier, afterwards dean of Luçon, whose father had been the confidential clerk and had succeeded to the practice of François de la Porte, Richelieu's maternal grandfather. Sebastien with his three brothers formed a small bodyguard of devoted adherents to Richelieu, and at every crisis of his early career we find a Bouthillier at his side. The dean of Luçon was an intimate friend of St. Cyran, and it was he who introduced him to another founder of the Jansenist sect, Arnauld d'Andilly. These four young men, Richelieu, the bishop of Poitiers, d'Hauranne, and Sebastien Bouthillier, formed a small association for the prosecution of theological study. Sometimes they met together at Poitiers, but when this was impossible they kept up a constant correspondence with each other.

But intimate as his connection was with these associates, Richelieu was careful not to commit himself to their opinions. His published letters prove that his aim at this time was to conciliate friends on all sides, and to quarrel with no one who could render him any service. He cultivated the acquaintance of Bérulle, the founder of the *Oratoire*, who established at Luçon the second house which his association possessed in

the kingdom. But the most important friendship which
he formed during his residence at Luçon was with
François du Tremblay, already known as a stern
monastic reformer, and afterwards famous as Father
Joseph, "the gray cardinal." Du Tremblay, who belonged to a noble family of Anjou, was eight years
older than Richelieu. Like him, he had been destined
for a military career, but at the age of twenty-two he
yielded to an irresistible religious impulse and dis-
gusted his family by becoming a Capuchin monk. He
became an active agent in the movement of ecclesiastical reform which characterised the first half of the
seventeenth century. Among the institutions which
were subject to his care was the famous abbey of
Fontevrault, near to which was the priory of Les
Roches, where Richelieu occasionally resided. In 1611
the abbess died, and Father Joseph wrote to the court
to secure the succession of Antoinette d'Orleans, who
had aided him in introducing much-needed reforms into
the abbey. Richelieu received instructions to supervise
the election, and it was this affair which brought
together the two men who were destined to be so
closely connected in the future.

Before this the death of Henry IV. had to some
extent modified Richelieu's plans of life. He realised
that the regency of Mary de Medici inaugurated a new
period in France, that retired merit would be of no
further use to him, and that in some way or other he
must thrust himself forward. He drew up a formal
oath of fealty, in which he and the chapter of Luçon
expressed their devoted loyalty to the king and regent.
This document was sent up to his eldest brother to be

presented to the queen-mother. But Henri de Richelieu,
who was a great person at court, and one of the mystic
"seventeen seigneurs" who aspired to set the fashions
of the day, rather scoffed at this exuberant profession
of fidelity, and suppressed the document, on the ground
that no one else had done anything of the kind. This
was not enough to discourage the aspiring bishop, who
determined in the future to make frequent visits to
Paris. He writes to Madame de Bourges to ask her to
find a private lodging for him. A furnished room, he
admits, would be more suitable to his purse ; but he
would be uncomfortable, and moreover he wishes to
make a figure in the world. "Being, like you, of a
somewhat boastful humour, I should like to be at my
ease, and to appear still more so ; and this I could do
more easily if I had a lodging to myself. Poverty is a
poor accompaniment for noble birth, but a good heart
is the only remedy against fortune."

Richelieu spent six months in Paris in 1610, and
though he did not obtain any employment, his time was
not wholly wasted. At the house of the Bouthillier he
made the acquaintance of Barbin, who held an influential
post in the queen's household. Barbin introduced him
to Concini, and thus established a connection with the
favourite, which enabled him five years later to enter
upon a political life. But at this time Concini, though
high in his mistress's favour, had not aspired to influence
the government, which was entirely in the hands of
Villeroy, Sillery, and Jeannin, the veteran ministers of
Henry IV.

Richelieu soon saw that his opportunity had not yet
come, and he again quitted Paris for his diocese. But

from this time he watched the development of events with ever-increasing interest, and he had made up his mind which side to take in the inevitable contest. The queen-mother had exhausted the treasures which Sully had amassed in bribes to the princes—she had given them offices, governorships, all that they demanded. By these means, and by dexterously playing off the Guises against the prince of Condé, she endeavoured to maintain at least the semblance of peace until the king should reach his majority, at the age of thirteen. But her concessions failed to conciliate the nobles, whose requests became the more insatiable the more they were granted. The ruling sentiment of Richelieu's career was his hatred of disunion and of princely independence. All his sympathies in the approaching struggle were with the court, with which he tried to draw closer the connection established in 1610. When the Huguenots in 1612 showed their discontent at the double marriage with Spain, and their leader, Rohan, made himself master of St. Jean d'Angely, Richelieu used his influence with the veteran Huguenot, du Plessis Mornay, to maintain order in his province, and wrote to the secretary of state, Pontchartrain, to assure him of his active co-operation.

His foresight had already perceived the means by which he was first to rise to power. He had no particular respect for Concini, who played a very vacillating part in the relations between the regent and the princes. But Concini's wife had that secure influence over Mary de Medici which comes from the habits of a lifetime, and the favourite might be a useful step in the ladder of promotion. At the beginning of 1614 the storm

seemed at last about to burst.   Condé and all the chief
nobles, except the Guise party, had withdrawn from
court and were collecting forces.   Concini himself, now
known as the marshal d'Ancre, who had intrigued with
Condé against the ministers, was in disgrace at Amiens.
Richelieu seized the opportunity to write to him the
following letter, dated February 12, 1614 :—

   "Always honouring those to whom I have once
promised service, I write you this letter to renew my
assurance, and to know if I can be of any use to you ;
for I prefer to testify the truth of my affection on important occasions, rather than to offer you the mere
appearance of it when there is no need : so I will use
no more words on this subject.   I will only beg you to
believe that my promises will always be followed by
fulfilment, and that, as long as you do me the honour to
love me, I shall always serve you worthily."

   On this occasion civil war was averted by negotiations,
and the treaty of St. Menehould was signed on May 15.
Once more the queen granted all that was asked of her.
Every confederate received something for himself, either
office, promotion, or money.   But among their demands
was one which was intended to express their devotion
to the public welfare—the summons of the States-
General.   This was also conceded, and the assembly
was finally summoned to meet at Paris in October.
The nobles had intended to use it as a means of
advancing their own interests, but they were disappointed.   The court succeeded in managing the
elections, and the vast majority of delegates were
devotedly royalist.   Richelieu was active in the cause ;
and the exertions of his three friends, the bishop of

Poitiers, Duvergier de Hauranne, and Sebastien Bouthillier, secured his own return as deputy for the clergy
of the province of Poitou. As soon as the *cahier* of his
order had been drawn up he carried it to Paris in
October.

He was now on the threshold of his public career,
and we may pause for a moment to consider the man
himself, before attempting to follow him through the
maze of intrigues in which he was so soon to be involved. His figure was tall and slight, but had not
yet contracted the stoop in the shoulders which
diminished his height in later years. His face was
long and pale, with a prominent and well-formed nose,
and surmounted by masses of long black hair. His lips
were thin and tightly drawn, at times relaxing in
a winning smile, but more often expressing stern
resolution. Perhaps his most striking characteristic
was a pair of bright penetrating eyes, under eye-
brows which were naturally arched as if to express
surprise. Clad in his purple bishop's robe, as he
appeared at the meeting of the States, he was the model
of an imposing ecclesiastic.

His great misfortune was his ill-health. During his
residence in the low, marshy district of Luçon he had
become liable to aguish fevers, which frequently
reduced him to absolute impotence of thought and
action. The energy with which he had thrown himself
into his theological studies and the administrative work
of his diocese had prematurely exhausted a frame which
had been feeble from infancy. He was subject to
excruciating headaches, which frequently lasted for days
at a time. On one of these occasions he registered a

vow, which has come down to us, and which shows the vein of superstition running through his imperious nature. If the Deity will cure his head within eight days, he promises to endow a chaplain with thirty livres a year to celebrate a mass every Sunday in the castle of Richelieu.

He was capable, as we have already seen, of inspiring warm feelings of friendship and devotion ; but his own nature was cold and reserved. His letters of condolence, even when he writes to his sister on the death of one of her children, are as measured and formal as a diplomatic epistle. Few human beings, except his favourite niece, could boast a secure hold upon his affection. Throughout his life he held himself aloof from ties that might bind and impede him. Political interests severed him from many of the friends of his early manhood, as, for instance, from St. Cyran, and he had no hesitation in sacrificing them for the success of his designs. He could appreciate devotion, but he could not return it.

Richelieu set out for Paris in 1614 with a resolute determination to carve out a career for himself. In his bishopric he had learned to exercise his powers, and had acquired confidence in them. He was no longer troubled with the self-distrust which had led to his retirement in 1608. He had spared no trouble to form connections wherever opportunity offered, but he had been careful to avoid entangling pledges. That he had at all made up his mind to carry through the vast schemes of his later life it would be preposterous to suppose. His ability was practical rather than theoretical. His policy was always to make use of circumstances, rather than to

attempt to wrest them to his wishes. His one firm
intention was to raise himself to political power ; and he
had the sublime confidence of every truly great man
that his own rule would be for the advantage of his
country.

CHAPTER II

THE STATES-GENERAL—RICHELIEU'S FIRST MINISTRY

1614-1617

Questions before the States-General—The *paulette*—Quarrels of
clergy and third estate—Richelieu orator of the clergy—Concini
and the ministers—Condé and the Huguenots oppose Mary
de Medici—Treaty of Loudun—Fall of the old ministers—
Richelieu rises to prominence—Conspiracy of the nobles—
Arrest of Condé and flight of his associates—Richelieu receives
office — His difficulties — Measures against the nobles—
Assassination of Concini—Fall of the ministers—Richelieu at
the Louvre—He quits the court.

THE States-General, which met on October 27, 1614,
are interesting as the last assembly held before the
famous meeting of 1789. In itself, however, it was
of very slight importance. The essential weakness of
these assemblies lay in the deeply-rooted class divisions
which ruined all prospect of constitutional government
in France, in the want of any practical check upon the
executive, such as is given in England by the control of
supply and expenditure, and in the tradition that their
only function was to formulate grievances. The great
questions raised at this meeting were the *paulette* and
the sale of offices, and the relations of the spiritual and
temporal powers. The nobles and clergy agreed to

demand the abolition of the *paulette*. The deputies of the third estate, most of whom belonged to the official class, were by no means eager for a change which would have deprived them of a valuable property. The instructions of their constituents, however, were too distinct for them to refuse their co-operation to the other estates, but they insisted upon complicating the question by demanding at the same time a diminution of the *taille* and a reduction of the lavish pensions granted by the crown. This last request was a direct attack upon the nobles, and a quarrel was imminent between the two estates, when attention was diverted to a new question.

The third estate demanded the recognition as a fundamental law that the king holds his crown from God alone, and that no power, whether spiritual or temporal, has the right to dispense subjects from their oath of allegiance. This at once raised all the thorny questions about the power of the papacy, which had been discussed with such vehemence in France for the last sixty years. The clergy hastened to resent the introduction of such a subject by a body of laymen, and to point out that the acceptance of the resolution would produce a schism in the Church. The support of the court secured them a complete victory. Mary de Medici had committed herself entirely to an ultramontane policy which was involved in the alliance with Spain. She had, moreover, a personal interest in the matter. An attack upon the supremacy of the pope would cast a slur upon the legitimacy of her own marriage, which rested upon a papal dispensation, and consequently upon the right of her son to wear the crown. The king evoked the matter to his own consideration, and the proposition was ultimately erased from the *cahier* of the third estate.

Emboldened by this victory, the clergy proceeded to demand the acceptance in France of the decrees of the Council of Trent, reserving the liberties of the Gallican Church. The nobles, irritated by the attitude of the third estate on the subject of royal pensions, hastened to support them. But the obstinacy of the third estate, more royalist than the court, succeeded in preventing the carrying through of a measure which France had persistently avoided for sixty years.

At last the *cahiers* of the three orders were completed, and were presented to the king in a formal session on February 23, 1615. We have, unfortunately, no record of the part played by Richelieu in the preceding debates, but that it must have been a distinguished one is proved by the fact that he was chosen on this occasion as the orator of his order. His harangue, which lasted more than an hour, is said to have attracted great attention. That it expressed his own personal views is improbable; many of its sentiments are in opposition to the whole tenor of his subsequent career. He seems to have conceived that his duty or his interest compelled him to act as the mere mouthpiece of the dominant majority, and to express opinions which he knew would be favourably received by the court. His whole argument is based upon the premises of ultramontanism. He condemns the practice of lay investiture, the attempt to levy taxes upon the clergy, whose only contributions ought to be their prayers, the interference with clerical jurisdiction, and the nonrecognition of the Council of Trent. Only two passages seem to express the personal convictions of the orator— his vigorous denunciation of the exclusion of ecclesiastics from the control of affairs, and his lavish praises of the government of the regent.

From this time Richelieu was a man of mark ; both Mary de Medici and Concini realised the value of the services which he might render to them, and his admission to political employment was assured.   Henceforth his residence in Paris becomes more continuous, and his diocese occupies less and less of his attention. For a long time Concini had been kept in the background by the close union among the ministers of the late king, whom the regent had never ventured to dismiss.   But this union had lately been weakened by a growing jealousy between Villeroy and the chancellor Sillery ; and the chief link between them was broken in November 1613, by the death of Villeroy's granddaughter, who had married Sillery's son, de Puisieux. The discord among the ministers was Concini's opportunity, and he determined to make use of it to get rid first of one section and then of the other.   His rise to power was accompanied by that of Richelieu.

In the autumn of 1615 it was decided that the court should travel to the Spanish frontier to complete the double marriage which had been formally agreed to three years before.   Condé and the other malcontent princes had given their approval to the marriages, but they now refused to accompany the court, and set to work to raise troops in their respective provinces. Regardless of the danger, Mary de Medici insisted upon continuing her journey to Bayonne.   Her eldest

daughter was sent to Spain to become the wife of the
future Philip IV., and Louis XIII. was formally married
to the infanta, Anne of Austria.   Meanwhile Condé had
collected an army, had evaded the royal troops under
marshal Bois-Dauphin, and had crossed the Loire into
Poitou.   At Parthenay he was met by deputies of the
extreme party of the Hùguenots, who had already
defied the royal authority, and the advice of their more
moderate leaders, by transferring their assembly from
Grenoble to Nîmes.   They now concluded a close
alliance with the oligarchical party, which pledged itself
to prevent the recognition of the Council of Trent, to
oppose the probable results of the Spanish alliance, and
to maintain the Edict of Nantes.   Thus the monarchy
was once more face to face with the forces of disunion.

Neither Concini nor Richelieu had accompanied the
court, and Mary de Medici was still surrounded by her
old advisers.   After some discussion in the council it
was decided to adhere to the well-worn policy of
negotiation and concession.   The office of mediator was
undertaken by the duke of Nevers and the English
ambassador, and their exertions resulted in the treaty
of Loudun, which was concluded in the spring of 1616.
The treaty marks a complete momentary victory for
the aristocratic party over the alliance between the
crown and the clergy, which had signalised the close of
the States-General.   The king promised to give a
favourable consideration to the demands of the third
estate, to reject the decrees of the Council of Trent, to
maintain the freedom of the Gallican Church, to respect
the privileges of the parliaments and other sovereign

courts, to uphold the existing alliance of France, many of which were opposed to Spanish interests, and finally to continue to the Huguenots all the concessions which had been granted to them by his predecessors. Secret articles stipulated for concessions to the individual princes, and the peace is said to have cost the king more than six million livres. Condé, who exchanged the government of Guienne for the more central province of Berri, was to be chief of the council, and was to sign all royal edicts.

The treaty of Loudun was followed by the fall of Sillery. As the chancellorship was, like so many other offices, a property for life, it was impossible to deprive him of it. All that could be done was to exile him from the court, and to intrust the seals to a keeper, du Vair, who had acquired a reputation as president of the parliament of Provence. But this first ministerial change was not enough to satisfy Mary de Medici or Concini. Before long Jeannin was deprived of the control of the finances, which was entrusted to Barbin. Villeroy was not absolutely dismissed, but he lost all influence. His colleague in the secretaryship of state, de Puisieux, shared the disgrace of his father, and his office was now given to Mangot, an ally of Barbin. Concini was prudent enough not to attempt to secure office for himself, but the ministers were in the habit of visiting him in his own apartments, and his vanity led him to magnify the extent of his influence over affairs.

The queen-mother had succeeded in freeing herself from the tutelage in which she had hitherto been kept by the veteran ministers of her husband, but her position was by no means secure nor satisfactory. Since

the majority of her son she had been far more eager for
power than she had been during the regency. One of
her most darling schemes, the Spanish marriages, had
been successfully completed. But she was confronted
by a powerful coalition of the chief princes, the third
estate, and the Huguenots, and she had been forced to
concede their demands at Loudun. When Condé came
to Paris he was apparently all powerful. His palace
was crowded, while the Louvre was deserted. Mary
was naturally anxious to turn the tables upon her
conquerors, and eagerly welcomed any assistance which
promised to contribute to her success. These circumstances gave Richelieu the opportunity for which he was
waiting. Whatever his personal opinions may have
been, he appeared before the world as the devoted
adherent of Mary de Medici and Concini, as the close
friend and ally of Barbin and Mangot. He succeeded
in obtaining the reward for which he was labouring.
Early in 1616 he was appointed almoner to the young
queen, Anne of Austria, and about the same time he
was admitted a member of the council of State. He
was employed on embassies to the prince of Condé and
to the duke of Nevers. In August a royal edict granted
to him an annual sum of 6000 livres "in consideration of the good and praiseworthy services which
he has rendered, and which he continues to render
every day." At this time it was intended to send him
as ambassador to Spain to settle a dispute which had
arisen in Italy with the duke of Savoy. But affairs at
home soon became too critical for him to be spared, and
the Spanish embassy was entrusted to somebody else.

The princes were unwilling to lose without a

struggle the advantages which they had secured at
Loudun. They were especially irritated by the influence
of Concini, a Florentine adventurer who had crept into
power by the favour of his wife. The court tried to
separate them by stimulating their ill-feeling against
Condé for having kept the lion's share of the spoil for
himself. But hatred of the foreigner was stronger than
their mutual jealousies, and in the autumn a general
conspiracy was formed against the favourite. Its most
active leader was the duke of Bouillon, the "demon of
rebellions," as Richelieu calls him, and with him were
combined Condé, the dukes of Mayenne, Guise, and
Nevers. It was the first time that the Guises and Condé
had been on the same side.

The coalition was extremely formidable, especially as
its hostility could not be limited to Concini. The conspirators felt, though Condé alone ventured to express
the general sentiment, that the overthrow of the
favourite would excite the bitter enmity of the queen-
mother, and that they would never be safe from her
vengeance unless they could succeed in separating her
from the king. But Mary de Medici, thus personally
threatened, was surrounded by very different advisers
to those who had counselled the shameful surrenders
of St. Menehould and Loudun. It was resolved to
paralyse the opposition by a bold measure, nothing less
than the arrest of Condé and as many as possible of his
allies. The scheme was carefully prepared, and the
secret was wonderfully kept, considering the number of
those to whom it was entrusted. Unfortunately, the
queen-mother's irresolution allowed the day to pass
which had been originally fixed, when most of the princes

were at the Louvre. Meanwhile, some suspicions were excited among the princes, but Condé was so confident in his power that he refused to entertain them. On September 1 he was arrested as he was leaving the council, and was at once imprisoned in a chamber of the Louvre.

The news struck consternation among the other nobles, who hastened to secure their personal safety by flight from Paris. As soon as they had recovered from their first fright, they held a conference at Soissons, where they agreed to raise troops in their respective provinces, to meet in twelve days at Noyon, and thence to advance upon Paris. Meanwhile, the prompt measures taken by the ministers had succeeded in preventing any serious outbreak in the capital, where Condé was extremely popular, and they set to work to sow dissension among their opponents. The Guises were soon detached from the coalition, and even the duke of Longueville was drawn over to the court by the influence of Mangot. Nevers and Bouillon, however, continued to hold out, and to prepare for civil war.

It is extremely probable, though there is no direct evidence, that Richelieu, as a member of the council, took part in the discussions which preceded the arrest of Condé. A vigorous policy was quite to his taste, and he had long been the intimate associate of Barbin, to whom, in his *Memoirs*, he attributes the chief part in these events. But one of the ministers, du Vair, was entirely out of sympathy with his colleagues. He had already proposed the release of Condé, and he now suggested calling in the parliament to settle the dissensions between the crown and the nobles. Such feebleness was intolerable. On November 25 the seals were taken from du Vair and given to Mangot. At the same time the secretaryship of state, held by the latter, was given to Richelieu, who, five days later, received a formal grant of precedence over the other secretaries. This completed the fall of Villeroy, who showed his resentment at being placed below his youthful colleague by ceasing to attend the council altogether.

Richelieu's first tenure of office only lasted for five months ; but during that period he succeeded in imparting to the actions of the government a firmness and consistency such as had not been witnessed since the death of Henry IV. He had many difficulties to contend with. The departments with which he was especially concerned were those of war and foreign affairs, and both were left to him in the greatest disorder. The regiments were below their proper numbers, the commissariat was wholly neglected, and the habits of discipline seemed to have been lost. Money was wanting for the soldiers' pay, and on this, as on several later occasions, Richelieu found it necessary to make large advances from his own funds. As for the foreign office, the most recent and important documents were missing. He had actually to write to the existing ambassadors for copies of the instructions that had been given to them. But perhaps the greatest difficulty of all was interposed by Concini himself, to whose favour he owed his appointment. The favourite's head had been turned by his rapid rise to power, and it was doubtful whether his insolence or his incapacity were the more conspicuous. Richelieu has preserved the fragment of a letter to Barbin, which illustrates the way in which he treated the ministers whom he regarded as his tools. "By God, sir, I complain of you that your treatment of me is too bad ; you negotiate for peace without consulting me ; you have induced the queen to urge me to abandon the suit which I have commenced against M. de Montbazon to make him pay what he owes me. By all the devils, what do you and the queen expect me to do ? Rage gnaws me to the very bones." France was weary of the caprices of a foreigner who had used his influence to amass riches and offices in his own hands. The ministers had reason to suspect that he was plotting to secure their dismissal, and Richelieu and Barbin actually offered their resignations to the queen-mother.

In spite of these obstacles, Richelieu and his colleagues succeeded in dealing the princes more severe blows than they had experienced at any previous period of the reign. Envoys were despatched to England, Holland, and Germany to remove any suspicions that might have been excited by the Spanish marriages, and to prevent any assistance being given by these powers to the rebels. The instructions to Schomberg, the ambassador to Germany, were drawn up by Richelieu himself, and contain the clearest exposition of the position and policy of the court. At the same time three armies were set on foot to act simultaneously in the Ile-de-France, Champagne, and the Nivernais. Everywhere the royal troops carried all before them. The eyes of Europe were fixed upon the siege of Soissons, where the duke of Mayenne was blockaded by the army under the count of Auvergne.

Suddenly the whole aspect of affairs was altered by

an incident which was entirely unforeseen. Concini's
unpopularity was a serious source of weakness to the
ministers ; but the fatal blow was struck from a quarter
from which it was least expected.   Hitherto Louis
XIII., who was only fifteen years old, had been regarded
as a mere cipher in the administration.   But the king
had his favourites as well as the queen - mother.
Prominent among these was a young man of obscure
origin, Luynes, whose chief recommendation was his
skill in falconry.   Mary de Medici and Concini had
taken him under their patronage, and had thought to
secure his allegiance by giving him the government of
Amboise.   But Luynes had ambitious designs of his
own which were by no means satisfied by the position
of personal favourite.   He persuaded Louis that
Concini purposely excluded him from affairs, that the
princes were perfectly loyal and were only alienated by
the omnipotence of the Florentine, and that the queen-
mother was influenced by a blind preference for his
younger brother, Gaston.   It was not difficult to persuade Louis to free himself from the galling yoke of his
mother's omnipotence by striking a blow against a man
whom he personally detested.   The plot against Concini
was arranged as secretly and successfully as that
against Condé.   No suspicions had been aroused in the
mind of the favourite when on April 24 he was arrested
on the bridge leading to the Louvre.   He had only
time to ejaculate, " I a prisoner ! " when he was killed
by three pistol bullets.   His captors excused their
precipitancy on the ground that he had offered
resistance.   All precautions had been taken.   The
queen-mother's guard was disarmed, and she found

herself a prisoner in her own apartments. Concini's wife was arrested, brought to trial, and executed. The body of the murdered man was disinterred by the mob, hanged by the feet on the Pont Neuf, dragged in hideous triumph through the streets, and finally burnt.

The news of Concini's death fell like a thunderbolt upon the ministers, who were expecting to hear every day of the fall of Soissons. Mangot was arrested, compelled to resign the seals, and then released as of small importance. Barbin, who was regarded as the chief agent in the late government, was strictly imprisoned. Richelieu alone was treated with some favour by the triumphant faction. He went boldly to the Louvre, where people who had courted him two hours before refused to recognise him. He found the young king raised upon a billiard table that he might be better seen by the crowd, and was assured both by him and by Luynes that they did not regard him as belonging to the faction of Concini. He was even granted admission to the council, where he found all the old ministers, Villeroy, Sillery, Jeannin, and du Vair in consultation. They received him with great coolness, and demanded in what capacity he appeared. On the answer that he came by special order of the king, they acquiesced in his presence, but he abstained from taking any part in the discussions, and soon afterwards retired. The change, however, was too complete and too sudden for him to retain his position, and he found himself compelled by necessity, if not by his own sense of gratitude, to follow the fortunes of the queen-mother.

CHAPTER III

THE death of Concini and the fall of Mary de Medici
seemed at first to effect a complete revolution. The
rebellion of the nobles was at an end; in fact, they
were received at court as if they had been fighting the
king's battles against his enemies. But they soon

discovered that the change of policy was not so complete as it appeared at first. They were jealously
excluded from the royal council. Condé, on whose
release they had confidently reckoned, was removed
from the Bastille to Vincennes, but his prison doors
were as securely guarded as ever. The nobles realised
that the ascendency of the king's favourite was as
intolerable as that of Concini. Nothing had happened
to reconcile the hostile interests of the monarchy and
the aristocracy.

The new government, though it had lost the opportunity of annihilating the power of the princes, was in
other respects not wanting in energy and decision.
Luynes, who took the chief conduct of affairs into his
own hands, was a far abler man than Concini. He
was determined to avoid the reproach of subservience
to Spain which had been cast upon the rule of the
queen-mother. French assistance was sent to the
duke of Savoy, which compelled the Spaniards to
withdraw their troops from Piedmont and to conclude
the treaty of Pavia. But at the same time a resolute
attitude was adopted towards the Huguenots. An
anomalous state of things existed in Béarn, which was
ruled by the French king without being united with
France. Henry IV., after his conversion, had restored
Roman Catholicism in his little Protestant kingdom ;
but he had left the church lands in the hands of the
Huguenots, while the Catholic clergy received their
stipends from the royal revenue. The French clergy
had never ceased to demand that the Church of Béarn
should be restored to its lawful possessions, and in
June 1617 a royal edict was issued to gratify this

demand. The Huguenots met at Orthez to protest, and the Parliament of Pau refused to register the edict. The struggle about its enforcement marks the beginning of the civil war, which ended in the loss by the Huguenots of their political independence.

Meanwhile Richelieu, with the permission of the king, had followed Mary de Medici into exile at Blois, where he was appointed president of her council. But he had many enemies at court, who persuaded the king that it was dangerous to allow him to remain in his mother's service. On June 15 he received a royal letter ordering him to reside within his diocese. He employed his compulsory solitude at the Priory of Coussay in composing a controversial work against the Huguenots. This took the form of an answer to four ministers of Charenton, who had replied to a hostile sermon preached before the king by Father Arnoux. The book itself is of slight merit, and its chief object was to keep the author prominently before men's eyes. It contains more vehement denunciations than arguments, and its intolerant tone is in marked contrast to Richelieu's own actions during his ministry.

The active defence of the orthodox creed did not suffice to secure Richelieu from the suspicions excited by his continued correspondence with the queen-mother. Coussay was considered too near to Blois, and early in 1618 he was exiled to Avignon, where he resided for a year. He was followed thither by his brother, Henri de Richelieu, and by the husband of his elder sister, de Pont-Courlay. So rigorous was the attitude of the court towards the family that Henri de Richelieu was not even allowed to pay a short visit to his home on the death of his wife. Richelieu, as before, solaced himself with the labours of composition. His new book, the *Instruction du Chrétien*, had a great vogue in his own lifetime, when it passed through more than thirty editions, but has since fallen into well-deserved neglect. French prose was not then the polished instrument that it became in the hands of Pascal and Fénélon, and Richelieu, in spite of his interest in literature, had little literary sense or capacity. The only occasions on which he wrote really well and pointedly were when his pen was inspired by scornful indignation. A letter which he sent about the end of 1610 to the grand vicars of Luçon is in its way quite a model.

During Richelieu's absence from court the ill-feeling against the administration of Luynes, in spite of the success of his anti-Spanish policy in Italy, was steadily increasing. He tried to conciliate popular opinion by abolishing the *paulette*, but the only result was to alienate the official classes, who represented that he merely wanted to make money by the sale of their offices. He showed no mercy towards his opponents, and thought he could rule by terror like an Italian prince. He did all he could in the trial of Barbin to induce the judges to sentence him to death, and when a bare majority refused to inflict a harsher penalty than exile, he persuaded the king to reverse his prerogative of mercy, and to commute the sentence to perpetual imprisonment. The queen-mother was treated with great severity at Blois; all her trusted servants were removed, and their places filled by nominees of Luynes, whose real functions were to act as spies upon her actions. At the same time his personal ambition was still more insatiable than that of

Concini had been. He married the daughter of the duke of Montbazon, afterwards famous as the duchess of Chevreuse. He extorted from Mayenne the important government of the Ile-de-France, to which he afterwards added that of Picardy. He was raised to the rank of duke and peer.

The great nobles were furious at this rapid rise of a man, whose father, as they said, was the bastard son of a canon of Marseilles and his chambermaid. In their jealous indignation they rallied to the support of the queen-mother, to whom they had so long been opposed. The chief agent in the negotiations was Rucelai, another of the numerous Italian adventurers who had been attracted to France by the marriages of French kings with ladies of the house of Medici. It was arranged that the queen should be released from prison, and that the duke of Epernon, the veteran champion of the nobles, should undertake the task of aiding her. In the night of February 21, 1619, she escaped from a window of the castle of Blois by means of a rope-ladder, and succeeded in making her way to Loches, where she was received by Epernon.

The escape of the queen-mother caused great consternation at court, and preparations were at once made for the civil war which seemed inevitable. At the same time the struggle might be averted if she could only be separated from the aristocratic party, with which circumstances had forced her into an unnatural alliance. Richelieu's old allies, Father Joseph and Sebastien Bouthillier, suggested that he was the very man for the purpose. He already possessed the confidence of Mary de Medici, and his influence would

serve to counteract the hot-headed counsels of Epernon
and Rucelai. Luynes, who had never shown such
hostility to Richelieu as others of his party, readily
adopted the suggestion ; and the sieur de Tremblay,
Father Joseph's brother, was sent to carry the necessary
instructions to Avignon. As Richelieu set out to obey
the order he was captured by a body of soldiers at
Vienne, but was at once released when it was known
that he had instructions from the king. He found the
queen-mother at Angoulême, where his arrival was
resented by the councillors, who sought to monopolise
influence over her. Richelieu's attitude during the next
two years has often been a puzzle to historians, but it
is really perfectly clear. The part which he had to
play was a difficult one, and he has frequently been
accused of betraying the queen-mother in the interests
of the court. But the charge is absolutely unfounded.
Devotion to Mary de Medici was rendered imperative
by his interest, as well as by his duty, but he was
under no such obligations to her associates. His clear
and unmistakable object was to separate his mistress
from the great nobles, and to effect her complete reconciliation with the king. He was conscious of a double
allegiance, to the queen-mother and the king, and he
displayed no common skill and dexterity in steering his
course when the two points to be aimed at seemed to
lie in opposite directions.

A personal quarrel between Epernon and Rucelai
induced the former to urge Richelieu's admission to the
council, which he had formerly opposed. His presence
gave a great impulse to the negotiations with the court,
and the treaty of Angoulême was hastily concluded on

April 30. A complete amnesty was promised to the adherents of Mary de Medici, and she resigned the government of Normandy for that of Anjou, with the towns of Angers, Pont-de-Cé, and Chinon. Normandy was given to the duke of Longueville in exchange for Picardy, which Luynes took into his own hands. The partisans of Rucelai were bitterly dissatisfied with the treaty, which they had done all in their power to prevent, and their discontent had disastrous consequences for Richelieu. The queen had entrusted the government of Angers to his eldest brother, who received a challenge from the marquis de Thémines, a member of Rucelai's faction. In the duel which followed, Henri de Richelieu was killed. This was a terrible blow to Richelieu, who was sincerely attached to his brother. The latter was a general favourite at court, and, in the judgment of Fontenay-Mareuil, he might, if he had lived, have rendered valuable services to the great cardinal.

The treaty of Angoulême was far from producing the results which Richelieu hoped. The dominant faction at the court remained bitterly hostile to the queen - mother. When she met her son at Tours, Luynes or one of his brothers was always present at their interviews, and succeeded in averting the restoration of her influence. The king set out to return to Paris, while Mary de Medici proceeded to Angers to take possession of her new government. The desired reconciliation was as far off as ever. The queen's adherents were treated with marked neglect or resentment. A new guardian, the Colonel d'Ornano, was appointed for her younger son, without even asking her opinion.

But the most direct blow was the release of Condé and the issue of a royal declaration in his favour, which virtually condemned the queen and all who had had a hand in his imprisonment. Richelieu in vain urged her to go to Paris, and to trust to the gradual revival of maternal authority over the king. She preferred to listen to the counsels of her more extreme followers, who wished her to remain at the head of the party of princes, and she demanded the dismissal of Luynes as an enemy of the state. It was the fear of this that had led to the release of Condé, in order that he might form a rival party among the nobles in opposition to the queen's adherents.

The year 1620 witnessed the outbreak of the civil war, which Richelieu had striven so desperately to avert. One after another the chief princes, Vendôme and his brother, Soissons, Longueville, Nemours, left the court with the avowed intention of resorting to armed force. Unfortunately all except Longueville hastened to join Mary de Medici at Angers, where they strengthened the violent opponents of Richelieu, while their jealous rivalry for the post of leader did much to weaken the cause which they had espoused. Their dissensions encouraged Luynes and Condé, now closely allied together, to take energetic measures. Carrying the king with them, they advanced into Normandy, where Rouen and the other chief towns surrendered in rapid succession, while Longueville fled to Dieppe without striking a blow. They then turned southward to confront the hostile coalition in Anjou. The most futile arrangements had been made by Vendôme and Marillac to resist the attack. Instead of strengthening the defences of Angers, which might have held out for months, they undertook to unite Angers and Pont-de-Cé by an entrenchment two leagues long, which they could not possibly complete in time, and which they had not men enough to defend, even if it had been completed. Richelieu pointed out the folly of the enterprise, but he was not in a position to insist upon his opinion, and it was probably rejected with scorn. The royal troops earned the position with an ease that was almost ridiculous. The rout of Pont-de-Cé became a byword in that generation. Vendôme himself was the first to carry the news to Mary de Medici, whose position was now hopeless. Richelieu urged her to cross the Loire and escape to Angoulême, where she could at least negotiate in security. But his advice was overruled by the cowardice of Vendôme and the countess of Soissons, and nothing remained but an unconditional surrender. Richelieu and the cardinal de Sourdis were entrusted with the negotiations on their behalf, and they were relieved to find that Luynes was ready to grant the same terms after the victory as he had offered before. The treaty of Pont-de-Cé contained no stipulations of any importance ; it professed to be nothing more than a reconciliation, a mutual promise that all injuries should be forgotten.

Richelieu's attitude in these events is clearly expressed in his assertion that the queen-mother "was saved from ruin by her defeat." If she had won a victory, all the fruits would have remained in the hands of the princes who fought for her. As it was, she was freed from all obligations to them, and the way was opened for the recovery of her influence at court. His most immediate object was to effect a real reconciliation

between Mary de Medici and Luynes, who was beginning
to resent the pretensions of Condé, and was not unwilling
to provide a rival to him in the person of the queen-
mother.   In the hope of effecting this purpose, Richelieu
agreed to a marriage between his niece, Mademoiselle
de Pont-Courlay, and the sieur de Combalet, nephew of
Luynes.   But the event disappointed his schemes, which
were destined to be carried through in a wholly unforeseen manner.

The escape of Mary de Medici and the events which
followed it had completely diverted attention from the
edict about church property in Béarn, which had never
been enforced.   After the treaty of Pont-de-Cé, Luynes
carried off Louis XIII. to suppress the resistance of the
Huguenots.   The campaign was soon over.   Navarreins,
the one fortress of the province, was compelled to
surrender, and the Roman Catholic clergy were placed
in possession of the ecclesiastical lands.   A royal edict
was issued to unite Béarn and Lower Navarre with the
crown of France.   Thus one of the great bulwarks of
Protestantism was destroyed, the work of centralisation
made a notable advance, and the king was received in
triumph on his return to Paris.

Meanwhile the French Huguenots had watched the
progress of events in Béarn with growing misgivings.
The leaders of the extreme party determined to antici-
pate attack by organisation.   In defiance of a royal
prohibition, they held an assembly at La Rochelle and
demanded the restoration in Béarn of the state of things
existing in 1616, the withdrawal of the garrisons
recently established in Guienne and Poitou, and the
satisfaction of the demands preferred in their last meet-

ing. The king offered to remove some of their grievances, but ordered the immediate dissolution of their assembly. This was urged by Lesdiguières and other moderate leaders; but they were powerless to control the more turbulent spirits, who believed that the divided court would never venture on active measures against them. In order to be prepared, however, for every danger, they proceeded to divide France into seven great provinces, in each of which there was to be a military commander and a provincial council. The supreme direction was to be entrusted to a commander-in-chief, who was to receive instructions from the general assembly at La Rochelle. As Bouillon refused the office and Lesdiguières was suspected on account of his relations with the court, the supreme command was entrusted to the duke of Rohan, the governor of St. Jean d'Angely. These preparations and the evident intention to form "a republic within the kingdom" excited the greatest indignation in Paris, and Louis XIII. determined to crush the rebellion by force.

Meanwhile Richelieu had failed to effect the desired reconciliation between Luynes and the queen-mother, and the latter was jealously excluded from the royal council. The marriage between Combalet and Mademoiselle de Pont-Courlay had been completed, but it had failed to produce any confidence between the two uncles. Luynes even took advantage of the marriage to endeavour to separate Richelieu from Mary de Medici, by giving out that the bishop of Luçon was now devoted to his interests, and that through him he was informed of all the queen's secrets. There were not

wanting advisers who urged Mary to renew her alliance
with the princes, and to try once more the chances of
war against the favourite.   Richelieu, however, was
eager to prevent a coalition which he had been at such
pains to break up, and he succeeded in persuading the
queen-mother to remain patient and to avoid hostilities.
This moderation enabled Luynes to embark in the
campaign of 1621.   In order to raise funds, he was
obliged to restore the *paulette*, and to raise a ruinous
loan on the security of the *gabelle* on salt.   At the same
time the office of constable, which had been vacant since
the death of Montmorency in 1614, was revived and conferred upon Luynes, although his military distinctions
were of the slightest.   In May the king with his army
entered Poitou, and after a short siege captured St. Jean
d'Angely.   After detaching Epernon to blockade La
Rochelle, Louis entered Guienne, and for a time carried
all before him.   These successes encouraged Luynes to
undertake the siege of Montauban, the chief Huguenot
stronghold in the south.   But here his good fortune
deserted him, and after serious losses had been sus-
tained he was compelled to raise the siege.   After the
death of du Vair, Luynes held the seals for a short time,
and this led Condé to remark that "he was a good
keeper of the seals in time of war, and a good constable
in time of peace."   His omnipotence had been tolerated
as long as he was successful, but his first failure led to
the outbreak of opposition.   Puisieux intrigued against
him in the ministry, but he was still strong enough to
maintain his position against attack.   To recover his lost
prestige he laid siege to Monheur, a fortress near Toulouse.
There he was seized by a fever, which carried him off

in four days (December 14, 1621). The reputation of Luynes has suffered from the unpopularity which dogs the footsteps of favourites ; but there can be no doubt that he deserves a more prominent place in history than has been usually allotted to him. He anticipated in some respects the future policy of Richelieu. He crushed a formidable coalition of the princes, and he inflicted the first serious blow upon the political independence of the Huguenots.

Richelieu and Mary de Medici had good reason to rejoice at the constable's death, but they soon found that all obstacles were not yet removed from their path. Condé and the ministers continued Luynes's policy of opposition to the queen-mother. Unable to prevent any longer her admission to the council, they did all they could to exclude her from any real control of affairs. The first subject of discussion in 1622 was the desirability of continuing the war against the Huguenots. Mary de Medici, expressing in council the opinions which Richelieu had drawn up for her, urged that civil war was rendered impolitic by the present condition of affairs in Europe, and that the primary duty of France was to check the growing power of the house of Hapsburg. But Condé, eager to separate the king from his mother, succeeded in persuading him to undertake a new campaign. The queen determined to follow him, but she fell ill at Nantes, and was compelled to retire to the waters of Pougues, whither Richelieu accompanied her. Meanwhile the king advanced into Poitou, where he defeated Soubise, Rohan's brother, and took Royan after a six days' siege. But for the second time he declined to attack La Rochelle, and leaving Soissons to cover the great stronghold of the enemy, he marched into

Languedoc. In order to restrain the growing pretensions of Condé, the constableship was given to Lesdiguières, who was thus induced to throw himself
altogether on the side of the crown, and to become a
convert to Roman Catholicism. The chief event of the
campaign was the siege of Montpellier, which was undertaken by Condé. But he was unsuccessful, and his
failure enabled the moderate party to induce the king
to agree to a peace. The treaty of Montpellier was
arranged between Lesdiguières and Rohan. The Edict
of Nantes was confirmed, but the Huguenots were only
allowed to retain two fortified places, Montauban and
La Rochelle. Condé was so indignant at the treaty,
which was signed without his having any knowledge of
it, that he left the court and set out on a journey to
Italy.

This year witnessed an important event in the life
of Richelieu—his elevation to the cardinalate. As early
as 1619 Mary de Medici had persuaded Louis XIII.,
when she met him after the treaty of Angoulême, to
demand this appointment from the pope. In the next
year, after the affair at Pont-de-Cé, she induced him to
write a second letter, and to send Sebastien Bouthillier
to Rome to urge the matter on the pope's attention.
For two years the faithful adherent of Richelieu remained at Rome trying to remove the difficulties in the
way of the nomination. The chief of these difficulties
arose from the resolute opposition of Luynes, and this
ended with his death, but Richelieu always suspected
the ministers of intriguing against his candidature. At
last Gregory XV. was induced to grant the coveted
dignity, and Richelieu received the news of his promo-

tion in September.   He went to Tarascon to thank the
king in person, and Louis, who seems never to have
regarded him with disfavour, told him that he could
not have succeeded as long as Luynes lived.

Richelieu had welcomed the conclusion of the treaty
of Montpellier as rendering possible a vigorous foreign
policy in opposition to the threatening power of Austria
and Spain.   But he was grievously disappointed.   The
withdrawal of Condé left the chief power in the hands
of Sillery and his son Puisieux, both experienced in the
conduct of affairs, but inclined by temperament to half-
hearted measures, and absorbed in the desire of maintaining their own authority.   Even the queen-mother,
so long devoted to the Spanish alliance, was at last
awakened to the dangers which threatened France, and
wished to abandon the vacillating policy which had so
long been followed.   This brought her into collision
with the ministers, who sought to strengthen themselves
by an alliance with the great nobles.   When Condé
returned from Italy they invited him to court in the
hope of playing him off against Mary de Medici.   But
they were destined to fall before the opposition of one
of their own supporters.   They had obtained the
removal of Schomberg from the control of finances, on
an unfounded charge of malversation, and his office was
given to the marquis of la Vieuville.   But la Vieuville
soon began to chafe at the subordinate position in
which he was kept by his colleagues, and intrigued
against them with the queen-mother.   The discovery
that considerable sums of money had passed through
the hands of Puisieux and had never been properly
accounted for, gave his enemies a handle against him

and his father. In January 1624 Sillery for the second time was driven from court, and the office of first minister passed into the hands of la Vieuville. But he soon realised that he possessed neither the experience nor the capacity to deal with the difficulties in which France was involved, and he looked round for assistance. His connection with Mary de Medici naturally suggested that he should have recourse to the ablest of her servants, but he feared that he would himself be over-shadowed by Richelieu's superiority. He proposed to form a council for foreign affairs, with the cardinal as president; but the members were to be excluded from the council of the king. Such a position was not likely to commend itself to Richelieu, and in April 1624 la Vieuville was compelled to advise the king to admit the cardinal to the council of state. Thus Richelieu entered office for the second time, and commenced an administration which was destined to be the most glorious in the history of France.

CHAPTER IV

THE VALTELLINE AND LA ROCHELLE

1624-1628

RICHELIEU, according to his own account, pleaded ill-health as an excuse for declining the burdensome responsibilities of office, but his scruples were overcome by the urgent entreaties of the king and the queen-mother, and on April 29, 1624, he was formally admitted to the council. La Vieuville, who regarded his new colleague with the jealousy of conscious inferiority, wished to subordinate him to the chancellor and the constable, but Richelieu insisted on the right of a cardinal to precedence even over princes of the blood. M. d'Avenel has published an interesting document, in which the new minister drew up a comprehensive scheme of internal reforms. The decrees of the Council of Trent were to be accepted, but without prejudice to the rights of the crown and the liberties of the Gallican Church. The monasteries were to be reformed and their number diminished, on the ground that they were a serious obstruction to industry. The expenses of the royal household were to be reduced by rigid economy. The *paulette* and the sale of offices were to be abolished, and on the death of existing office-holders the number of places was to be diminished. To relieve the people, the *gabelle* on salt was to be reformed so as to fall upon foreigners rather than upon subjects, and the exemptions from the *taille* were to be cut down in number and refused in the future. Provincial governments were only to be held for three years, and all useless fortifications were to be demolished.

If Richelieu had carried out these reforms he would have deserved the lasting gratitude of France. But they represent the pious wishes of a newly-appointed minister rather than the matured intentions of an experienced statesman. Possibly many of the changes would have been repudiated by Richelieu himself in later years; but at the moment his attention was

distracted from domestic affairs by the overwhelming
pressure of foreign politics. Since the death of Henry
IV. the policy of opposition to the house of Hapsburg
had been abandoned, with fatal results to France. In
the great war which began in Germany in 1618 the
emperor and the Catholic League had won a series of
victories. Not only was the Bohemian revolt suppressed,
but both the Upper and the Lower Palatinate had been
conquered, and in 1623 they were transferred, with the
electoral vote, to Maximilian of Bavaria. Ferdinand
II., as the champion of the Counter-reformation, held a
stronger position in Germany than any of his predecessors
since Charles V., and he threatened to become stronger
still, if once he could form an army of his own, and thus
free himself from dependence upon the Catholic princes.
Still more serious for France was the progress made by
the neighbouring power of Spain, the close ally of the
emperor. Philip IV. and Olivares were reviving the
ambitious aims of Philip II. Their troops, under
Spinola, had reduced the Lower Palatinate, and they
now threatened to conquer the United Provinces, which
could hardly make an effective resistance without support.
England, which under Elizabeth had been a champion
of Protestantism, and which had special reasons for
sympathy with the Elector Palatine, was paralysed by
the fatuous policy of James I., who allowed himself to
be fooled by the prospect of marrying his son to the
Spanish infanta. Unless resolute steps were taken,
Spain threatened to shut France in altogether on her
eastern frontier by a chain of dependent or subject
territories. Negotiations had been opened with Vienna
for the surrender of Tyrol and Elsass to the Spanish

crown.   And finally Spain attempted to evade the
Alpine barrier which shut off her Italian territories
from her possessions in Central Europe.   In 1622 her
troops had seized the important pass of the Valtelline,
which connected Lombardy with Tyrol, in defiance of
the claim of France to control the valley.

Sillery and Puisieux had fallen because they had
failed to check the aggressions of Spain, and the task
was now intrusted to la Vieuville and Richelieu; but
they were hampered by serious difficulties in their way.
France was a Roman Catholic country, and Richelieu
was a cardinal of the Church.   Though he might be
willing to subordinate religious to political interests,
and though he defended this by the example of the
Roman court itself, yet he could not afford to give
Spain the advantage of posing as the champion of the
orthodox creed.   Moreover, in France itself there was
a strong Ultramontane party which resented any rupture
with Spain, and Richelieu's patroness, Mary de Medici,
would hardly pardon such a complete change of attitude
as would appear to condemn her conduct during the
regency.   Above all, it was imperative not to entangle
France in foreign relations which might advance the
interests of the Huguenots.   Thus alliances with Protestant powers could only be half-hearted, and accompanied
with reservations fatal to their efficiency.   Vigorous
intervention in Germany, perhaps the best method of
checkmating the schemes of Spain, was impossible,
because it would alienate the Catholic League, which
it was Richelieu's intention to conciliate, in the hope
of playing the princes off against the emperor.   The
attempt to recover ascendency in the Valtelline was

rendered difficult by the necessity of keeping on good
terms with Rome, and of securing the Catholic inhabitants
of the valley from oppression by their Protestant rulers.

Through these difficulties, which were not diminished
by the absence of a good understanding with his principal
colleague, Richelieu steered his way with a mixture of
caution and resolution which does more credit to his
intellect than to his convictions.   France hastened to
renew its alliance with the Dutch, which had been
broken off since Henry IV.'s death, and to welcome
the overtures made by England.   Buckingham's journey
to Madrid had resulted in breaking off the proposed
Spanish marriage, and James I. now demanded the
hand of Louis XIII.'s sister, Henrietta Maria, for the
Prince of Wales.   The negotiations were long and
tedious.   Richelieu's claim to precedence as a cardinal
being disputed by the English envoys, he feigned illness,
and received them in his bed.   But the great difficulty
arose from the French demand that James should promise
toleration to the English Roman Catholics, as he had
offered to do in his negotiations with Spain.   The English
king was willing to give a verbal promise, but France
insisted upon a formal and binding agreement, counter-
signed by an English minister.

During the negotiations the differences between
Richelieu and la Vieuville became more and more
manifest.   The latter assured the English envoys that
the demand for toleration was a mere form to satisfy
the pope and the French Catholics, and that Louis
XIII. really cared nothing about the matter.   The king,
who considered that his honour compelled him to exact
at least as favourable terms as had been proffered to

Spain, was furious at this attempt to frustrate his wishes. In August la Vieuville was dismissed, and Richelieu was left without a rival in the ministry. His superior tact and determination enabled him to score a diplomatic triumph. The English court, urged on by the reckless Buckingham, agreed to make the desired stipulation, and to be satisfied with the barren concession that it should not form part of the marriage contract. Father Bérulle was sent to Rome to procure the papal dispensation, and the marriage was celebrated in the spring of 1625, soon after Charles I. had succeeded to the throne on his father's death.

If Richelieu, as he gives out in his *Memoirs*, was the guiding spirit throughout this transaction, his policy is open to serious criticism. Buckingham wished France to assist Mansfeld in the recovery of the Palatinate. Richelieu, on the other hand, was determined not to entangle himself in Germany, but wished to involve England in a war with Spain, in order to divert Spanish attention from the Valtelline. His trump card in the negotiations was the knowledge that Buckingham was resolved on the French alliance, and that Buckingham dominated both James and Charles. This enabled him to make the alliance on his own terms. But it was extremely foolish, from the political point of view, to exact such concessions to the Roman Catholics. Not only were causes of quarrel certain to arise from so one-sided an agreement, but it necessarily involved the English court in a quarrel with the parliament, and without the supplies of parliament English intervention on the continent was sure to be futile. Possibly Richelieu may not have appreciated the importance of

the parliamentary aspect of the matter, but it is more
probable that he was not a free agent, and that the line
which he took was forced upon him. It was not in his
power to acquire all at once that ascendency over the
king which he afterwards established, and in this question
of the English marriage the real decision rested with
Louis and his mother. If Richelieu had attempted to
oppose them he would have shared the fate of la
Vieuville.

France had been driven to renew her Protestant
alliances in Europe, mainly by events in the Valtelline.
This important valley, which runs from Lake Como into
Tyrol, was the property of the three Grison leagues,
which themselves formed part of the Swiss Confedera-
tion. Ever since the reign of Louis XII. the Grisons
had been the allies of France, and had pledged themselves to close their Alpine passes against the enemies
of that country. But for some time the Spanish governor
of Milan had been endeavouring by intrigues and threats
to secure the control of the Valtelline, and in 1603 the
fort of Fuentes had been built at the entrance of the
pass. Since then a Spanish party had grown up in the
Grisons, and had set itself to oppose the dominant
influence of France. In 1620 this party organised a
revolt of the Roman Catholic population of the Valtelline against the oppressions of the judges appointed
by the Protestant leagues. The Spaniards aided the
rebels in expelling the Swiss troops that were sent
against them, and four forts were constructed in the
valley and garrisoned by Spanish troops. The Grisons
now appealed for assistance to France, and a French
envoy negotiated the treaty of Madrid (April 25,

1621), by which the forts were to be destroyed, and everything restored to its former condition. But the outbreak of the Huguenot war encouraged the Spaniards to evade the fulfilment of the treaty, and in 1622 the Grisons, attacked simultaneously from Austria and from Milan, and despairing of French aid, made terms with Spain, by which they renounced their sovereignty over the Valtelline, and agreed to grant a passage to Spanish troops. The conclusion of the treaty of Montpellier at last enabled Louis XIII. to turn his attention to affairs in Italy, and in February 1623 he formed a league with Venice and Savoy to compel Spain to carry out the treaty of Madrid. The Spaniards, who were not prepared to embark in a new war, now agreed to submit the dispute to the arbitration of the pope, and the forts were handed over to papal troops under the command of the marquis of Bagny. But Urban VIII., although personally inclined to oppose the domination of Spain in Italy, was unable to resist the pressure of the Spanish party in Rome, which urged the impiety of restoring Protestant rule in the Valtelline. The terms which the pope proposed were so favourable to Spain that they were unhesitatingly rejected by Richelieu, who at last decided on energetic measures. In the winter of 1624 the marquis de Cœuvres, who had been sent on an embassy to the Swiss cantons, was ordered to raise troops for the reduction of the Valtelline. The attack was entirely successful; the papal garrisons were taken unprepared, and early in 1625 the valley and the forts were completely in the hands of the Swiss and the Grisons. At the same time, in order to divert the attention of Spain, the constable Les-

diguières was sent to co-operate with the duke of
Savoy in an attack on Genoa.

But Spain could count on efficient supporters within
France. No sooner had the government embarked in a
foreign war than Huguenot discontent broke out into
open rebellion. The Huguenots, who were still headed
by Rohan and Soubise, complained that the treaty of
Montpellier had not been carried out, and especially
that the fortifications of Fort St. Louis, which threatened La Rochelle, had been strengthened instead of
being destroyed. In January 1625 Soubise, who had
already seized the island of Rhé, suddenly attacked and
captured the royal vessels in the harbour of Blavet.
This success was the signal for a general rising ; La
Rochelle espoused the cause of Soubise, and Rohan took
up arms in Languedoc. The court was panic-stricken
at the news, and a majority of the council wished to
conclude a peace with Spain at any price. All Richelieu's
firmness was needed to prevent an abject surrender of
French interests in Italy. The great difficulty in the
way of suppressing the Huguenots was the want of
ships, and Richelieu resolved to obtain them from the
Protestant powers. Both England and Holland were
furious with the Huguenots for threatening to ruin the
grand combination against Spain, and they promptly
agreed, not only to supply vessels, but to allow France
to man them with French captains and troops. Montmorency took command of the fleet and won a complete
victory over the rebels, who were driven from Rhé and
Oléron. Soubise fled to England, and the Huguenots
hastened to sue for peace.

It was at this time that Christian IV. of Denmark

undertook the championship of the Protestant cause in Germany. Richelieu considered that Spain, involved in hostilities with the English and Dutch, and pledged to the assistance of the emperor, could not act with energy in Italy, and that a very moderate effort would compel her to concede to the French demands. He therefore made use of English mediation to conduct negotiations with the Huguenots. This policy excited the bitter hostility of the Ultramontane party, who resented the collision with the papacy even more than the breach with Spain. This party was now headed by Bérulle, and it was supported within the council by Marillac, the controller of finance, and afterwards keeper of the seals. Virulent pamphlets were published against Richelieu, in one of which he was stigmatised as the "cardinal of la Rochelle." To conciliate his opponents, who might at any moment be strengthened by the adhesion of the queen-mother, he was compelled to authorise the comte du Fargis, the French ambassador at Madrid, to open negotiations with Olivares. But du Fargis allowed himself to be gained over by the Ultramontanes, and in January 1626, without authority, he signed a treaty with Spain. Richelieu, who saw clearly that powerful influences were at work in the matter, and who feared the alienation of Venice and Savoy, insisted on repudiating this treaty, and also another which du Fargis signed at Monzon on March 5. The final treaty, modified to suit the interests of France, was not signed till May 10 at Barcelona, but it is usually known in history as the treaty of Monzon. The sovereignty of the Valtelline was to be restored to the Grisons. Spain abandoned all claim to control the passes, and the forts were to be again handed over to the pope and destroyed.

Meanwhile the English ambassadors, ignorant of the events in Spain, were urging on the negotiations with the Huguenots, in order that France might be able to act with energy in Italy.   Thanks to their exertions the Huguenots were induced to withdraw their demand for the destruction of Fort St. Louis, and to accept a very disadvantageous treaty on February 5.   But, from the point of view of the government, the treaty had one very serious defect—that it was based upon English mediation. Charles I. had revenged himself for Louis's intervention on behalf of the Roman Catholics.   The Huguenot deputies declared that they would never have accepted the treaty but for pressure from England, and for the assurance that henceforth "they might lawfully accept assistance from the English king."

For the moment, however, Richelieu seemed to have triumphed. He had humbled the Huguenots with the help of their natural allies, and he had forced Spain to resign her hold upon the Valtelline.   But his very success had served to stimulate discontent at home.   All the interests which dreaded the growth of a strong monarchy combined against the minister who threatened to destroy all restrictions upon royal absolutism.   Even before peace was concluded rumours began to circulate of approaching changes in the government.   The personage upon whom all eyes were turned was the king's younger brother, Gaston, whose succession to the throne seemed almost inevitable, since Louis's health was feeble and his marriage had proved for many years unfruitful. But Gaston himself was not very formidable ; he was only the tool of those who surrounded him.   The real contrivers of the plot were the marshal d'Ornano, whom

Richelieu himself had released from prison and restored to his former office as governor to Monsieur, and the duchess of Chevreuse, the widow of Luynes, who had since married a member of the house of Guise. It is difficult to ascertain their precise objects ; probably they had never distinctly formulated them themselves. Their overt measures were to demand the admission of Gaston to the council, and to oppose the plan of marrying him to Mademoiselle de Montpensier. Rumour accused them of having further designs : to remove Louis XIII. to a monastery, to place Gaston on the throne, and to marry him to Anne of Austria. The latter is said to have exclaimed in answer to the charge, "I should not have gained enough by the change." It is certain, at all events, that the conspiracy was directed against Richelieu, whose removal was a necessary preliminary to any further measures. Nearly all the princes were more or less involved : Condé, because he resented his continued exclusion from the court ; the young Soissons, because he wished to secure the Montpensier inheritance for himself ; the rest from a general desire to increase their own importance and independence. To the Frenchmen of the seventeenth century a plot was an attraction itself ; they did not need any carefully-prepared schemes or skilfully-dangled bribes to induce them to embark in it. According to Richelieu, foreign powers were also implicated. England, Holland, and Savoy all resented the conclusion of the treaty of Monzon, and were willing to overthrow the statesman whom they considered responsible ; while Spain was always on the look-out for the opportunity of stirring up domestic disorder in France.

The plotters seemed to have talked with a reckless indiscretion, which had been natural enough under the feeble regency, but which was madness now that power had fallen to a man capable and willing to use it. Richelieu waited till he had collected enough evidence to satisfy the king, and then struck with vigour and decision. On May 4, Ornano was seized and imprisoned at Vincennes, where he died four months later. Gaston went in a rage to the cardinal, who firmly accepted the responsibility for the action. To most of the conspirators little severity was shown. The king's half-brothers, the duke of Vendôme and the Grand Prior, were taken prisoners, and Madame de Chevreuse, exiled from the court, escaped to Lorraine. Condé hastened to come to terms with the government, and the other princes were treated with passive contempt. Gaston, who was formally reconciled with Louis and his mother, received the duchies of Orleans and Chartres as an appanage, and Richelieu himself officiated at his marriage with Mademoiselle de Montpensier. But while a politic clemency spared the leaders, one of their tools was selected for condign punishment, as an example of the dangers of conspiring. Henri de Talleyrand, count of Chalais, whose mother had bought for him the office of master of the wardrobe, had been drawn into the plot by the seductive charms of the duchess of Chevreuse. His youthful indiscretion had led him into foolish conversations, which were now brought up against him. He was tried before a specially appointed commission, and was condemned to be beheaded and quartered. In spite of the frantic supplications of his mother, the sentence was carried out. That he was more or less guilty there is little doubt;

but he was far less to blame than others who escaped, and his untimely fate will always excite a feeling of indignation against the ruthless policy which chose him as a sacrifice.

The inevitable result of this abortive conspiracy was to strengthen the minister against whom it was directed. The king granted Richelieu a bodyguard of a hundred men, to protect him against the malice of his enemies. His control over the government became the more absolute as it appeared that he was the necessary bulwark of the royal power. At this moment the constableship was left vacant by the death of the veteran Lesdiguières, and Richelieu seized the opportunity to suppress an office which gave excessive authority and independence to its holder. The corresponding office of admiral was purchased from Montmorency for 1,200,000 livres, and was also suppressed. Thus the army and navy were brought under the direct control of the ministers, and a great step was taken in the process of centralisation. Richelieu himself was profoundly impressed with the necessity of making France a great naval power, in order to protect and extend French commerce, and to avoid the humiliation of depending for foreign assistance against Huguenot rebellion. To give him the necessary authority, the king conferred upon him the novel office of " grand-master, chief, and superintendent-general of navigation and commerce." Large sums of money were raised to build and purchase ships, and to furnish them with crews and necessary stores. As a navy in those days must be based upon a large mercantile marine, Richelieu projected the formation of a great company at Morbihan, which should dispute the trade with the East and West Indies, with England, Holland, and Spain.

Richelieu's measures were not only dictated by a wise comprehension of the future interests of France : his gaze was never long withdrawn from the immediate drama of foreign affairs. The Protestant cause in Europe, with which France could not but be intimately connected, had suffered severe blows in 1626. Christian IV. of Denmark had been crushed by Tilly and the troops of the Catholic League ; Mansfeld had been irretrievably defeated by the imperial army under Wallenstein. To make matters worse, England, which was more responsible than any other power for the failure of the Danish king, and which had failed in its own naval attack upon Spain, did not hesitate to add to its difficulties by picking a quarrel with France. The marriage contract of Henrietta Maria had produced nothing but quarrels and misunderstandings between the two powers. Charles I. could not grant the promised toleration to the Roman Catholics in face of parliamentary opposition, and so he calmly repudiated his promise and allowed the penal laws to be enforced. He quarrelled with his wife for her avowed partiality for her native country and her own religion. So far did his anger carry him that he expelled with insult the French ladies and priests of the queen's household. He resented the maritime schemes of Richelieu as an encroachment upon the naval supremacy which he claimed as England's right. English cruisers captured French vessels on the slightest pretext, and their cargoes were sold by order of the English courts as contraband of war.

So far as these disputes constituted causes of war, it was France which had most cause of complaint. But indignant as Louis XIII. and Mary de Medici might be at the treatment of Henrietta Maria and the shameless disregard of the marriage contract, they would have been restrained by Richelieu from endeavouring to redress their grievances by arms. It was England which embarked upon the war, and her conduct was so obviously fatuous under existing circumstances that men were at a loss to account for it. The real author of the French war, as of the French alliance, was Buckingham. When he had visited France to escort Charles I.'s bride to England, he had been audacious enough to make open love to Anne of Austria, the neglected wife of Louis XIII. Since then he had several times suggested his return to Paris as envoy for the settlement of disputes, but his proposal had always been rejected by the king and queen-mother, who had no desire that he should carry his insolent overtures any further. Contemporaries did not hesitate to assert and to believe that the proud favourite considered himself insulted, and that he revenged himself by attacking France. It is more probable that he wished to conciliate the hostile majority in parliament, who had never forgiven him for allowing English ships to be employed against the Huguenots. With a sublime self-confidence, which no failure had been able to weaken, he believed that his enterprise would be irresistible, and that a rapid success would give him a position in England which nothing could shake. Although the Huguenots were not in revolt, he announced himself as the champion of their interests, and complained that the recent treaty

had been broken by the retention of Fort St. Louis, and
by the construction of the two forts of St. Martin and
La Prée on the island of Rhé, which commanded the
entrance to the harbour of La Rochelle.   No pains were
spared in fitting out the fleet, which sailed from Stokes
Bay on June 27, 1627.   Its exact destination was at
first uncertain, but on July 10 it anchored off the coast
of Rhé.   Two days later the troops were landed after
a stubborn struggle, and proceeded to lay siege to the
fort of St. Martin.

It was a critical moment in the career of Richelieu.
Louis XIII. was ill with a tertian fever, and the
cardinal did not dare to leave him.   Yet upon him fell
all the responsibility of resisting an invasion, which had
been foreseen but very insufficiently provided against.
And the English were not the only enemies to be
considered.   Rohan, urged on by Buckingham, hastened
to raise once more the standard of revolt in Languedoc.
La Rochelle was at first inclined to resent an enterprise
about which it had never been consulted, and to remain
obstinately neutral.   But it was certain that the
citizens would be forced before long to espouse the
English cause.   And Buckingham had made careful
preparations to divert the attention of France.   His
envoy had gained over Charles IV. of Lorraine, at
whose court the duchess of Chevreuse continued her
incessant intrigues against Richelieu.   The discontented count of Soissons was at Turin, and both Savoy
and Venice only waited for the news of an English
victory to join the coalition against France.   And
within France itself there were many opponents of the
cardinal who would have welcomed a defeat which

should discredit his administration. He had no ally to look to except Spain, with whom France had concluded a treaty in April. But it was notorious that Spain only desired to embroil France with England, and that Olivares had actually revealed the treaty to Buckingham in order to induce him to accept his terms. The most immediate danger, however, was in the island of Rhé. Toiras, the commander, had received lavish grants of money, but had neglected to hurry on his preparations. Neither of the two forts was in a condition to resist attack, and at the moment of his landing Buckingham might have carried either of them by assault. But he paid no attention to La Prée, and wasted four days before reaching St. Martin. His delay enabled the garrison by great exertion to complete the defences just in time, and the English were compelled to abandon the assault for a blockade. This gave the French time to organise the relief of the fortress; but the matter was still urgent. Toiras had barely food enough to last two months, and his needs were increased when Buckingham collected the mothers, wives, and daughters of the garrison, and drove them into the fortress by a volley of English bullets. As the English naval force was superior to any that France could bring against it, and as the assailants must sooner or later have the co-operation of La Rochelle, it seemed as if the surrender of the fort was only a question of time.

But Richelieu's energy rose to the occasion. Though he spent the whole day and many nights by the king's bed, and was compelled to disguise his anxieties for fear of alarming the patient, he undertook the whole super-intendence of the necessary measures for the relief of St.

Martin.   He had the capacity, which seems peculiar to
great statesmen, of grasping every minute detail as
clearly as the general outline of a scheme.   Nothing
was too small for him, and he shrank from no labour or
responsibility.   The duke of Angoulême was appointed
to command the army in Poitou, with instructions to
watch over La Rochelle and prevent any assistance being
given to the English.   Before long it was found necessary to extend this supervision to a regular siege.
Agents were sent in every direction to collect sailors,
ships, and provisions, at the ports of Brouage and the
Sables d'Olonne.   Special care was taken to provide a
number of pinnaces and rowing-boats from Bayonne, so
that the relieving force might be independent of the
wind, and might evade the shallows of a low tide.
Succour was sent to the island of Oléron, which was
more fertile than Rhé, and which would become of
immense importance if the latter were lost.   The Spanish
offers of assistance were accepted, though Richelieu had
little confidence in their good faith, and the subsidy
treaty was renewed with the Dutch, so as to secure at
least their neutrality.   As the treasury was wholly unable to meet the extraordinary expenditure, Richelieu
employed his own money and his own credit to supply
the deficiency.

Before the end of August the king was well enough
to travel, and he and Richelieu at once set out to join
the army before La Rochelle.   Their arrival did much
to stimulate the exertions to assist the besieged fort, but
though some few supplies had been smuggled in,
nothing substantial had been achieved.   The garrison
was more and more pressed by want, and on Sep-

tember 25 an offer of surrender was actually made, but postponed to the next day. That very evening the wind took a favourable turn, and the relieving force succeeded in making its way through the English fleet, with the loss of only one boat. St. Martin was safe for nearly six weeks. For the moment the English were so discouraged as to decide on abandoning the enterprise, but the promise of speedy reinforcements induced them to change their mind. But the English administration was hopelessly corrupt and inefficient, and Charles's good-will was not enough to fit out the ships in time, or to provide favourable winds when they were ready. Meanwhile the besiegers were suffering from the inclemency of an early winter, and found themselves in danger of being in their turn besieged. Richelieu had succeeded in sending troops across to the island, where they found a safe shelter in the neglected fort of La Prée. It was known that Toiras could not hold out beyond November 5, but Buckingham could not hold out so long. On October 27 he made a futile attempt to storm the fort, and two days later he proceeded to embark his troops. But Marshal Schomberg brought up the newly-arrived soldiers from La Prée, and the English retreat was turned into a confused and ruinous rout. Buckingham returned to England with barely a third of the force that had accompanied him. Some three weeks later the Spanish fleet, which a little before might have rendered invaluable services, arrived at Morbihan.

The English invasion had forced Richelieu into a closer alliance with the ultra-Catholic party than he would have formed of his own accord, and he found it advisable to cement the alliance by inducing the pope to give the cardinal's hat to Bérulle, though the latter was his avowed rival for the favour of the queen-mother. The full extent of the dangers which threatened France had been recently revealed by the papers of Montague, the English envoy, who had been captured on the borders of Lorraine. These disclosed, not only the intrigues of Buckingham with Lorraine, Savoy, and the count of Soissons, but also a design on the part of the emperor to assert his claim to the bishoprics of Metz, Toul, and Verdun, which had been occupied by France since 1553, but had never been resigned by the Empire. Some documents found in Buckingham's camp at St. Martin also revealed the intrigues of Spain with England. But Richelieu determined to disregard as much as possible these external dangers, and to concentrate his attention upon the siege of La Rochelle. The task of making head against Rohan in Languedoc was entrusted to Condé, a notorious hater of the religion which his fathers had professed, and to Montmorency, the governor of the province. The king and cardinal set to work to form an efficient blockade of the Huguenot stronghold in the west. The three commanders of the army, Angoulême, Schomberg, and Bassompierre, undertook to close all access to the town by land by the construction of a line of fortifications, three leagues in length, which were defended by eleven forts and eighteen redoubts. But relief from the land side was little to be dreaded, and the most serious problem was to close the entrance to the harbour. This was the special care of Richelieu himself. Acting on the advice of two French engineers, he ordered the construction of two great moles, one from each side of the harbour, at a sufficient distance from the town to be out of range of cannon-shot. The moles were to be built of huge stones, with a slope on each side, so as to break the force of the waves. In the middle a space was to be left for the tide to go in and out, but this was to be partially blocked by sunken ships, and to be guarded by the French fleet. In January this fleet arrived from Morbihan under the command of the duke of Guise, and with it came the Spanish vessels which had professed to come for the relief of St. Martin. But they had scarcely been eight days at anchor when a false report of the approach of the English compelled the Spaniards to show their true colours, and to demand leave to depart. The officers themselves were ashamed of the part which they had to play, and which they vainly tried to excuse on the ground of necessary preparation for a joint attack upon England in the summer.

Richelieu had other difficulties to contend with besides the fury of the winds, the heroic obstinacy of the besieged citizens, and the aid which was promised to them by England. All whose interests were opposed to the strengthening of the monarchy looked forward to the fall of La Rochelle with serious misgivings. Bassompierre only expressed the prevalent sentiment of his class when he exclaimed, "We shall be fools enough to take the city." The most careful supervision and the exercise of sovereign authority were needed to prevent careless or treasonable neglect of the siege operations. It was, therefore, a heavy blow to him when he learnt that Louis XIII., weary of the monotony of camp life, and dreading the winter climate on the salt marshes, announced his determination to return to Paris. At first he risked the royal displeasure by opposing the king's wishes, and when he had to give way, he found it necessary to offer an opportunity for the intrigues of his opponents by consenting to remain at La Rochelle. Fortunately Louis was capable of appreciating his devotion. Not only did he entrust Richelieu during his absence with the supreme command by sea and land, but he resisted the attempts of his mother to prolong his stay in the capital, and in April had once more returned to the siege.

Richelieu had now the opportunity of displaying the military tastes and capacity which he had developed in his younger days. Attired in a garb which betrayed the soldier rather than the ecclesiastic, he undertook the personal direction of the siege works by land and sea. The strictest discipline was maintained, and the cardinal triumphantly compared his camp to a well-ordered monastery. The men were well paid, well fed, and well clothed—a striking contrast to the condition of most of the armies of that period,—and the amount of sickness was surprisingly small. Steady progress was made with the moles, though the ravages of the sea more than once made it necessary to do much of the work over again; but each time some lesson was learnt and some fault of construction was remedied. Richelieu had good reason for energetic action, when he heard that the queen-mother had joined the ranks of his opponents, and that war had broken out in Italy about the succession to Mantua and Montferrat. Twice he tried to surprise the town during the night, but both attempts failed, and he had to trust to the slow but certain results of the blockade. The return of the king removed some of his ˋworst anxieties, but he was still worried by the urgent necessity of relieving Casale, which was besieged by the Spaniards. He could, however, do nothing till La Rochelle had fallen. In May an ˙English fleet under Lord Denbigh sailed to relieve the town, but it was ill-equipped, and the sailors were the discontented victims of impressment. After viewing the defences of the harbour, and upbraiding the deputies from La Rochelle for their false information, the English retired without striking a blow, but promising that they would return with a stronger force. Meanwhile the besieged were reduced to the greatest straits. The supplies of food were carefully reserved for the fighting men; the women and children, and all who could not bear arms, were forced to support a miserable existence on roots, shellfish, and even boiled leather. At last the useless mouths were driven out, but the king sternly refused to let them pass, and many died of starvation between the walls and the royal lines. Nothing but the iron resolution of the mayor, Guiton, prevented an immediate surrender, when the news came that Buckingham, just as he was preparing to start for their relief, had fallen a victim to Felton's knife. This event delayed the expedition, but it sailed in September under the command of the earl of Lindsay.

It was now too late. The two moles had been
completed, and the gap between them had not only
been filled with sunken vessels, but was also guarded
night and day by a number of ships fastened together
in the shape of a half-moon. The only chance was
to make a way through by means of fire-ships, which
had once been so successful at Antwerp. But the
fire-ships were ill-directed, and were grappled and
towed to shore by French boats. The English
attack was a failure. Charles vainly tried to negotiate
on terms which might have been possible before
Buckingham's repulse from Rhé, but which were
preposterous now that the fall of La Rochelle was
inevitable. The citizens at last realised that their
cause was hopeless, and on October 28 they agreed
to capitulate, on condition that their lives should be
spared, and liberty of worship allowed to them.
Richelieu's influence over the king was strong enough
to prevent the attack upon a rebellious city from
being converted into a crusade against heresy. Two
days later the triumphal entry took place. The three
marshals marched abreast to avoid any disputes as to
precedence, then came the cardinal alone, and then
the king. Richelieu appeared on that day as the
first subject of France. On the city of La Rochelle
fell the punishment from which the citizens were
spared. Its walls were destroyed, its municipal
privileges were cancelled, and no Protestant who had
not been born there might take up his residence in
the town. Even the fortresses of St. Louis and St.
Martin were to be razed to the ground, as there was
no longer any need for their existence.

Thus Richelieu had lived to achieve the scheme which he had dreamed of when he was simple bishop of Luçon. He had humbled the last municipality which was capable of resisting the power of the monarchy. To him, more than any other man, was the victory due, and his wise moderation had prevented its being abused in a way that would have produced lasting disaffection and disunion in France. The capture of La Rochelle was the achievement to which, in his later years, he looked back with the greatest pride and the most unalloyed satisfaction.

CHAPTER V

THE MANTUAN SUCCESSION AND THE DAY OF DUPES

1628–1631

LA ROCHELLE had fallen, but Casale was still holding out.
It was not yet too late for Richelieu to resume that
policy of opposition to Spain which the quarrel with
England and the revolt of the Huguenots had compelled

him for a time to abandon.   He had allied himself with
the Ultramontane party, but he was not their slave.   To
their intense disgust he again postponed the annihilation
of Rohan and the Huguenots in the south, while he
concentrated his attention upon the maintenance of
French interests in Italy.   The question of the Man
tuan succession requires a few words of explanation.

Vincenzo di Gonzaga, who had succeeded two of his
brothers as duke of Mantua and marquis of Montferrat, died without issue on December 26, 1627.   His
nearest male heir was Charles of Gonzaga, duke of
Nevers, a French subject, and governor of the French
province of Champagne.   But though female succession
was excluded in Mantua, it was lawful in Montferrat,
and to prevent the separation of his territories, the late
duke had married his niece, Mary, to Nevers's son, the
duke of Rethel.   In January 1628 the duke of Nevers
took possession of his inheritance, to which his legal
claim was unquestionable.   But Spain, the dominant
power in Italy, was determined to prevent the establishment of French influence within that country.   Encouraged by the prospect of Spanish support, various
claimants came forward to oppose the succession of the
French duke.   The duke of Guastalla, also a descendant
of the Gonzagas, laid claim to Mantua on the ground
that the Nevers family had forfeited its rights by
having borne arms against the emperor.   The duchess
of Lorraine, sister of the three last dukes, maintained
the legality of female succession in Montferrat, and
Charles Emmanuel of Savoy advanced an old claim of
his family to the same province.   The emperor Ferdinand II., urged on by Spain, asserted his right as suzerain

to settle these disputes, and in the meanwhile ordered the provinces to be handed over to his commissioner, John of Nassau.

The new duke of Mantua, trusting in support from France, refused to obey this order, and the Spaniards at once undertook to enforce the imperial authority. They were most immediately interested in Montferrat, which they regarded as a bulwark of the duchy of Milan. The alliance of Savoy was easily purchased by the promise of considerable territories in Montferrat, and Don Gonzales, governor of Milan, led an army to the siege of Casale, the chief fortress of the province. Nevers, hardly established in Mantua, could not hope to resist the combined forces of Spain and Savoy. France, occupied in the siege of La Rochelle, could not interfere effectually in Italy, and a small force which was sent under the marquis of Uxelles was repulsed at the entrance into Piedmont. Fortunately a small body of French volunteers had thrown themselves into the citadel of Casale, where the defective skill and vigilance of the besiegers enabled them to maintain themselves until the fall of La Rochelle set Richelieu and the royal army at liberty.

Although the season was extremely ill-suited for such an enterprise, Richelieu determined to cross the Alps for the relief of Casale, and if possible to take the king with him. Mary de Medici, who cherished an old grudge against Nevers, and disapproved of the expedition altogether, did all in her power to induce her son to stay in Paris. But Louis XIII. had tasted the sweets of martial glory before La Rochelle, and the success of his arms had inspired him with enthusiastic confidence

in the cardinal. On January 15, 1629, they quitted
Paris together, and after travelling through Champagne
they reached Grenoble on February 14. No other
minister accompanied them, Schomberg having fallen ill
at Troyes, and the whole burden of making preparations
for the campaign fell upon Richelieu. The administrative system in the provinces was extremely corrupt
and inefficient, and only the most authoritative supervision could secure that orders should be punctually
carried out. But the cardinal's energy vanquished all
obstacles, and on February 22 the king set out from
Grenoble for the pass of Mont Genèvre. Charles
Emmanuel sent his eldest son, who had married
Louis's sister, to negotiate, but Richelieu discovered
that the negotiations were merely intended to procure
delay while the intrenchments on the Italian side of the
pass were being strengthened. The order to advance
was given, and the French attack carried all before it.
The intrenchments were forced, and on March 3 the
king entered Susa in triumph. This vigorous action
brought the duke of Savoy to reason, and the prince of
Piedmont was again sent to arrange terms with Richelieu.
The treaty of Susa was signed on March 11. The
duke promised to give the French passage through his
territories, and to furnish supplies for the relief of Casale.
As security for the fulfilment of his promise Susa was
to be left in French occupation. He also undertook for
Don Gonzales that the Spaniards would retire from
Casale and Montferrat, that they would abstain from
any further acts of hostility against the duke of
Mantua, and that the confirmation of these terms by
Philip IV. should be obtained within six weeks. Louis,

on the other hand, promised to procure for the duke the
town of Trino and other lands in Montferrat to the
value of 15,000 crowns, as the price of the renunciation
of his claims.   At the same time Richelieu drew up a
projected league for mutual defence between France, the
pope, Venice, Mantua, and Savoy.   Charles Emmanuel
undertook to adhere to this league when it had been
joined by the other states.

The prompt action of the French had thus secured
for them a second military triumph within six months.
The Spaniards could not hope to resist the royal army,
and Don Gonzales was compelled to accept the terms
which Charles Emmanuel had arranged for him.   Casale
was relieved, and there was yet plenty of time left to
reduce the Huguenots.   Louis XIII. set out from Susa
in April to commence this task.   Richelieu remained
behind to watch the duke of Savoy, who was too veteran
an intriguer to be trusted to fulfil his engagements of
his own accord, but on May 19 the cardinal was able to
join the king before Privas, the Protestant stronghold
of the Vivarais.   He had already dealt a crushing blow
to the Huguenots by concluding a treaty with England.
Charles I. abandoned the cause of the rebels, who had
been led to rely upon English assistance, and Louis
withdrew his demand for the restoration of Henrietta's
household.   Rohan, who had foreseen the defection of
England, had sought compensation in an alliance with
Spain, and the Most Catholic king had not hesitated
to sign a treaty with the leader of Protestantism in
France.   If any had been needed, this treaty would
have supplied ample justification to Richelieu for his
determination to crush the Huguenots.   It provided

that if they succeeded in forming an independent state, they would grant toleration to Roman Catholic worship. The possibility of such an ideal being entertained was enough to convince Richelieu that he must strike boldly and decisively if he wished to effect that unity of France which was the ultimate object of all his exertions.

Before Spanish assistance could arrive the blow had been struck. Privas was taken soon after Richelieu's arrival, and sacked with all the horrors of war. This severity, which the cardinal in his *Memoirs* maintains to have been unintentional, was as effective as if it had been deliberately planned. The Vivarais submitted, and the king entered the Cevennes, offering amnesty and toleration to all who submitted, and to those who resisted the fate of Privas. The alternative was irresistible, and one town after another opened its gates. The rebellion had collapsed, and the Huguenot deputies hastened to accept the terms which were offered to them, not as a treaty between equals, but as an act of grace from a sovereign to his subjects. The Edict of Nantes was confirmed, but the political privileges which had been granted at the same time by supplemental edicts were cancelled. The Huguenot fortifications were to be razed to the ground, and there were to be no more "towns of surety." Freedom of worship and of individual belief was granted, but it was granted as a royal favour which could at any time be revoked. Henry IV. had not been strong enough to enforce toleration by the royal authority, and had been forced to place weapons of self-defence in the hands of the Huguenots. Thanks to Richelieu, the monarchy could now afford to dispense with such precautions, and could

thus revoke privileges which its own weakness had
rendered necessary, and which had been used against
itself. The danger of the formation of "a state within
the state" was at an end. The only misfortune was
that Richelieu could not ensure that the monarchy
should always be tolerant.

After a triumphal entry into Nîmes, Louis XIII. set
out for Paris on July 25. Richelieu remained behind
to obtain the submission of Montauban, only second to
La Rochelle as a Huguenot fortress, to supervise the
destruction of the fortifications, and to put an end to
the administrative independence of Languedoc. It was
not till September 14 that he was able to rejoin the
king at Fontainebleau. He soon found that he had to
confront difficulties at court quite as serious as those
which he had coped with abroad. Gaston of Orleans
had never been well disposed to Richelieu, whom he
accused of a deliberate scheme to exclude him from all
voice in public affairs. He was still the puppet of a
small group of interested associates, who wished to use
him as a catspaw for their own advancement. His first
wife had died in childbirth, and he was anxious to
marry Mary of Gonzaga, the daughter of the duke of
Mantua. This was opposed both by his brother and
mother; and Mary de Medici, during the king's absence
in Italy, went so far as to imprison the princess Mary
at Vincennes. Gaston then demanded an increase of
his appanage, and the government of some important
provinces, such as Champagne and Burgundy. Louis
was so jealous of his younger brother that Richelieu's
advice was not needed to convince him of the danger
of handing over frontier provinces to a discontented

heir-apparent. Gaston, however, attributed the refusal to the influence of the cardinal, and loudly demanded his dismissal. When Louis returned from Languedoc, Gaston refused to meet him at court, and retired to Champagne. There he professed to believe that he was in personal danger, and proceeded to Lorraine, where Charles IV., always willing to harass the French government, received him with open arms.

Still more formidable to Richelieu was the open hostility displayed to him on his arrival by Mary de Medici. For the last three years the relations of the queen-mother and her former servant had been growing more and more strained, and the chief causes of her ill-will are not difficult to trace. Throughout her life Mary de Medici was guided rather by passion than by policy. She cherished strong likes and dislikes, but they were directed against persons, not against principles. She had learnt to regard Richelieu as a creature of her own, who owed his advancement to her patronage, and she was chagrined to find him acting in complete independence of her wishes. She intended to keep her elder son entirely under her own control, and she discovered, to her dismay, that the cardinal's influence over Louis was stronger than her own. The guiding thread to the tortuous labyrinth of her caprices is to be found in a steady attachment to dynastic interests, and especially to those of her three daughters.

This brought her into direct collision with the cardinal's policy, which was dictated solely by a regard to the interests of France. Her eldest daughter was the queen of Spain, and Richelieu was the arch opponent of that power. Another daughter was married into the

house of Savoy, and Mary de Medici would gladly have
supported its claims to Montferrat. But Richelieu had
actually carried Louis off to Piedmont, had humiliated
the duke of Savoy, and had forced him to resign his
claims in favour of the duke of Nevers, whom she
hated, both for his past career, and because he wished
to become the father-in-law of her younger son. The
third daughter was the wife of Charles I., and her
interests—so her mother thought—had been completely
sacrificed in the last treaty with England. After the
interests of her family, Mary de Medici was most
solicitous for the interests of religion, and these were
specially urged upon her at this time by her most
intimate advisers, Cardinal Bérulle and Michel Marillac.
They wished for a general alliance of Catholic against
Protestant states, for the maintenance of a good understanding with Spain, and for the persecution of the
Huguenots at home. But their aims were not those
of Richelieu. If political reasons rendered it advisable,
he was as willing to ally himself with Holland or
Sweden as with Bavaria or Austria. He had ample
experience of the hollowness of Spanish promises, and
of the resolution of the court of Madrid to do all in its
power to weaken France by stimulating internal discord
and encouraging foreign enemies. He may also have
been actuated by a sentiment of personal rivalry against
the Spanish minister, Olivares, who certainly entertained
that feeling towards Richelieu. Finally, he had reduced
La Rochelle and Languedoc, but Bérulle, a bigoted
mystic, could not pardon him for having left the heretics
in enjoyment of religious toleration.

Against the hostility of the queen-mother, based

upon personal, dynastic, and religious motives, Richelieu was not without supporters. Mary de Medici, as in the days of her regency, had connected herself with the Guise party at court. Her favourite confident was the princess of Conti, a sister of the duke of Guise. She made up her former quarrel with her daughter-in-law, Anne of Austria, also a vigorous hater of Richelieu, and opened a connection with the queen's exiled favourite, Madame de Chevreuse, whose husband was a Guise. The duke of Guise himself had a personal quarrel with Richelieu because he claimed the command in the Mediterranean as pertaining to his governorship of Provence, whereas the cardinal held that his office gave him control over all maritime affairs in every sea. But the old antagonism between the Guises and the princes of the blood—a dominant factor in the history of the later part of the sixteenth century—still subsisted, and the cardinal could oppose to the queen's partisans the support of Condé, who had become his enthusiastic admirer since the siege of La Rochelle, and of the count of Soissons, who had now returned to France, and had made up his quarrel with the government. His only real security, however, lay in the hold which he had acquired over Louis XIII. Richelieu was no favourite, in the proper sense of the word. He did not rise to power, like Buckingham, by personal favour, nor did he retain it by flattering his master and humouring his foibles. But he was a favourite in the sense that every minister of a despotic sovereign must be a favourite. He could not hold his office if he forfeited the king's confidence or incurred his serious displeasure. Circumstances had brought him into Louis XIII.'s service, and he had so

employed them as to make himself indispensable.
Much has been written, in contemporary memoirs and
in later histories, of the ascendency acquired by Richelieu
over the king, and of the jealous hatred which Louis
entertained against the minister, whose superiority he
resented, but whom he dared not thwart or dismiss.
Much of this can be proved by documentary evidence
to be an exaggeration of the cardinal's enemies.   Louis
XIII. was rather timid than weak, and his moral
cowardice made him eager to say what would please
the person he was talking to.   He was also slow and
hesitating in his speech, and he was often unable to
find words to answer the violent expostulations of his
mother, or the voluble entreaties of his wife.   His
silence was easily interpreted to imply what he had no
intention of expressing, for under his apparent weakness was concealed considerable obstinacy of opinion
and purpose.   He really shared his minister's devotion
to the aggrandisement of France in Europe and the
increased authority of the monarchy.   Probably they
often differed as to the means which were to be
employed, and the cardinal's superior abilities doubtless
enabled him as a rule to convince and persuade the
king ; but there were several occasions when Richelieu
found it advisable to give way, and any temporary
resentment which Louis may have entertained was
more than removed by the success which attended their
joint exertions.   It is impossible to prove that Louis
loved his minister, but he respected him, and he loved
nobody.

The coldness with which the queen-mother received
Richelieu at Fontainebleau was too obvious to escape

the notice of a curious court. Richelieu met the hostility of his former patroness by offering his resignation—a favourite weapon in the hands of a minister conscious of his fidelity and of the merit of his services. Louis, who "wept bitterly for nearly a whole day" on account of his mother's importunities, refused to accept the resignation, and issued letters - patent conferring upon the cardinal the formal dignity of "principal minister of state." Mary de Medici was compelled to swallow her indignation, and she was the more willing to postpone her desire for vengeance as the death of Bérulle—whom Richelieu was absurdly accused of poisoning—deprived her of one of her most trusted advisers. Richelieu now set himself to arrange terms with Gaston of Orleans, whose residence at a foreign court was a glaring proof of French dissensions, and an encouragement to the enemies of France. Months were wasted in the attempt to satisfy the jealous prince and his ambitious councillors, and it was not till January 1630 that the offer of an increased appanage induced Gaston to return to France, though he still refused to see his brother or to appear at court.

Meanwhile Richelieu discovered that he ran the risk of losing all that he had achieved by his march to Piedmont. The emperor, elated by his victories over the German Calvinists and their Danish champion, was furious at the attempt of France to settle the succession to imperial fiefs without any regard to his authority. He looked on the treaty of Susa as an insult, and withdrew a considerable number of his troops from the north to vindicate his suzerainty in Italy. In the spring of 1629 the imperial army entered the Grison

territory and proceeded to occupy the Valtelline and
other passes. After some time had been spent in
negotiations, the imperial general, ·Colalto, descended
into the Lombard plain. Philip IV. and Olivares were
eager to seize the opportunity for resuming the schemes
which they had been forced for the moment to abandon.
The unconquered Spinola was sent to supersede Don
Gonzales in the government of Milan. While the
Imperialists advanced upon Mantua, where the duke
himself was shut up, Spinola led the Spanish troops
into· Montferrat and again threatened Casale, which was
now defended by a French garrison under Toiras, the
hero of St. Martin.

France could not allow Spain and the empire to
triumph in Italy, and the despatch of a new army was
an obvious necessity. But who was to lead it? The
expedition involved diplomatic as well as military
difficulties, and their solution could not safely be
trusted to a subordinate. Richelieu, of course, was
anxious not to leave Louis XIII. to resist unaided the
influence and intrigues of Mary de Medici and her
partisans. On the other hand, he could hardly venture
once more to expose the still childless king to the
hardships and dangers of a winter campaign. Moreover
the treaty with Gaston was not yet finally settled, and
there was danger of an attack from Germany on the
side of Champagne. In the interests of France
Richelieu was compelled to risk his personal security.
On December 29, 1629, he set out from Paris with
powers such as have rarely been granted to a subject.
He was appointed "lieutenant-general, representing the
person of the king with his army both within and

without the kingdom." He had authority to receive
and send envoys, and to conclude or reject treaties.
Under him served Marshals Créqui, Schomberg, and
la Force.

The passage of the Alps was effected without opposition, though not without considerable loss, and in the
first week of March the French army reached Susa.
Richelieu had made up his mind not only to fight the
battles of the duke of Mantua, but also to secure some
fortress at the foot of the Alps that would enable
France at any time to interfere decisively in Italy.
He had no intention of falling into the error of Louis
XII. and Francis I., and of attempting to make France
the mistress of Italian provinces, but he meant to strike
a blow at Spanish domination, and to gain the confidence of those Italian states which still retained a
shadow of independence. The great difficulty in his
way was the attitude of Savoy. If Charles Emmanuel
had been willing to fulfil the treaty of Susa, it would
have been impossible to pick a quarrel with him, and it
was only at his expense that the desired fortress could
be acquired. But the wily duke played into the
cardinal's hands. His one idea was to involve France
and Spain in open hostilities with each other, and to
make his own profit by selling his support to the
highest bidder. He offered to aid the French, if they
would join him in attacking Milan and Genoa, and
would promise not to lay down arms till both had been
conquered. This Richelieu refused, as he did not wish
for an open rupture with Spain, and desired that
France should continue to play the part of an
auxiliary and not of a principal in the war. Then the

duke offered to remain neutral, and to supply provisions for the French. This Richelieu at first accepted, in order that Casale might obtain ample supplies to resist a blockade. But he soon discovered that Charles Emmanuel was also negotiating with Spinola and Colalto, and that he was strengthening the intrenched camp which he had formed at Avigliana, between Susa and Turin, as a barrier against the French advance. Richelieu now decided to abandon negotiations, and to turn his arms against his treacherous ally, as it would be madness to advance upon Casale with a hostile Piedmont in his rear. On March 19 the French army advanced against Rivoli, where Charles Emmanuel had his headquarters. An eye-witness has described the cardinal's appearance as he crossed the little river Dora at the head of the troops. "He wore a blue cuirass over a brown coat embroidered with gold. He had a feather round his hat, and two pages marched before him on horseback, one carrying his gauntlets, the other his helmet. Two other pages marched on either side of him, and each held by the bridle a valuable charger; behind rode the captain of his guards. In this guise he crossed the river on horseback, with his sword at his side and two pistols at his saddle-bow. When he had reached the other side he made his horse caracole a hundred times in presence of the army, boasting aloud that he knew something of this exercise." In spite of all this martial pomp, the assault on Rivoli failed to effect the desired capture of the duke and his son, who escaped to Turin. But instead of advancing upon the capital of Piedmont, the French suddenly returned towards the Alps and invested

Pinerolo, a fortress commanding the exit of the chief pass from Dauphiné. Pinerolo, which had been held by France for a considerable period in the previous century, was compelled to surrender on March 30, before the duke of Savoy had time to relieve it.

The capture of Pinerolo was a terrible blow, not only to the duke of Savoy, but also to the Spaniards and Imperialists, whose chief dread was that the French might obtain a permanent footing in Italy. They at once offered to negotiate, and Urban VIII. undertook the office of mediator. It was on this occasion that Giulio Mazarin, who was employed as a papal agent, first attracted the notice of Richelieu, whose service he afterwards entered, and whom he eventually succeeded as first minister in France. The negotiations came to nothing, because the one essential condition of peace was the cession of Pinerolo, and Richelieu had no intention of resigning his conquest except in the last necessity. But so far he had done nothing for the duke of Mantua, and Spinola and Colalto were already preparing to resume the sieges of Casale and Mantua, which had been abandoned during the winter. The cardinal conceived the bold plan of saving these fortresses by an invasion of Savoy. If the Spaniards and Imperialists advanced to the aid of their ally, they would have to postpone their enterprises in Montferrat and Mantua. If they did not, the duke of Savoy would be compelled to come to terms, and this would render possible the despatch of an army to relieve Casale. If the worst came to the worst, and both Mantua and Casale fell, France would have something substantial in hand to offer in return for their restitution.

On May 2 Richelieu left the army at Pinerolo under Schomberg and la Force, and hurried to Grenoble to meet Louis XIII., who had undertaken to conduct the invasion of Savoy. The king had started in the company of his mother and his wife, both of whom disapproved of the expedition, but he had left the two queens at Lyons. From Grenoble the king and cardinal advanced into Savoy, and their operations were conducted with the good-fortune which had always attended their joint presence. Chambéry surrendered after a siege of one day, and in June the whole duchy had been reduced, with the exception of the single fortress of Montmélian. The natural sequel to this success was an advance to the relief of Casale, which was now closely besieged by Spinola. But the outbreak of pestilence in Piedmont made it impossible for Louis XIII. to enter Italy, and Richelieu's position was now so directly threatened by the queen-mother and her adherents that he dared not risk another period of absence from the king. The bulk of the royal army was despatched on July 6 under Montmorency and d'Effiat across Mont Cenis, and they succeeded, after a sharp contest with the troops of Charles Emmanuel at Avigliana, in effecting a junction with the army which had been left at Pinerolo. The marquisate of Saluzzo was now conquered by the French, but their success was more than counterbalanced by the news that Mantua, which the Venetians had undertaken to relieve, had been stormed on July 17, and that the Imperialist forces were free to advance to the aid of Spinola. Charles Emmanuel, whose intrigues had resulted in the loss of the greater part of his dominions, died on July

26, but his successor, Victor Amadeus, though less committed to an anti-French policy, could not free himself at once from the obligations which his father bequeathed to him. France, therefore, gained nothing directly from the change of rulers. Meanwhile Casale was being hardly pressed, and Toiras announced that he could not hold out much longer without assistance. If Richelieu could have come to Italy in person, the threatened fortress might have been relieved, but the cardinal was more than ever absorbed by the king's ill-health and the machinations of his enemies. In his absence, the French marshals were afraid to run the risk of a bold and decisive march, and their troops were harassed by sickness and bad weather. Under these circumstances Mazarin was at last able to arrange a truce at Rivalta on September 4. Hostilities were to be suspended on all sides until October 15 ; the town and castle of Casale were to be handed over to the besieging army, who were to supply provisions for the interval to the garrison of the citadel. After October 15, if peace had not been concluded, the French army might resume its advance, but Toiras pledged himself to surrender if relief did not reach him before October 30. Spinola, who was lying on his deathbed, refused to abandon his prey by signing the truce, but it was accepted by the duke of Savoy and Colalto, and the death of the veteran general three days later removed all difficulties, as his successor pledged himself to observe the stipulations.

It was fortunate for France, in its quarrel with the emperor and with Spain, that Richelieu had not relied solely upon the achievements of the French arms in

Italy. His gaze embraced the whole field of European politics, and he knew how to make the most various and distant circumstances subserve his immediate aims. It was the retirement of Christian IV. of Denmark from the German war which had enabled the emperor to send an army against Mantua. But Richelieu had already made preparations to bring another prince on the stage to take the place vacated by the Danish king. Gustavus Adolphus, the young and energetic king of Sweden, had many motives for hostility to the emperor, and he was eager to defend the cause of Protestantism and to extend the power of Sweden on the Baltic coasts. He had already thwarted Wallenstein's attempt to take Stralsund, and nothing but his dynastic quarrel with the Polish king prevented him from throwing himself into Germany. Here was Richelieu's opportunity. Early in 1629 a French envoy, Charnacé, had been despatched to the northern courts. He succeeded in negotiating a ten years' truce between Poland and Sweden, and he drew up a projected treaty of alliance between Sweden and France. Thus Gustavus Adolphus was able to enter Germany in the next year without leaving his own territories exposed to invasion, and with the additional advantage that a large contingent of the emperor's troops was engaged in Italy.

Still more skilful were the combinations of Richelieu's policy in Germany. The victories of Wallenstein had raised the power of the empire to a height which had not been reached for more than three centuries; but at the same time they had weakened the alliance between the emperor and the Catholic League. Maximilian of Bavaria and his associates had fought to humiliate the

Protestants; but they had no intention of sacrificing their princely independence to the domination of Ferdinand II. and his haughty general. They demanded the dismissal of Wallenstein and the disbandment of his army. It was in vain that Ferdinand tried to conciliate them by issuing in 1629 an edict ordering the restitution of all ecclesiastical possessions which had been occupied by Protestants since the great religious peace of Augsburg. The only result was to alienate the Lutheran princes, who had been the most loyal adherents of the empire, and who were forced against their will to form an alliance with Sweden. The Catholics continued to persist in their demands, and their opposition, carefully stimulated by Richelieu, brought matters to a crisis at the diet of Ratisbon, which Ferdinand summoned in June 1630, to procure the election of his son as king of the Romans. Richelieu sent Leon de Brulart as French ambassador to the diet, and with him went the cardinal's *alter ego*, the famous Father Joseph. Their intrigues were crowned with complete success. At the moment when Gustavus Adolphus landed on the coast of Pomerania, Ferdinand was compelled to dismiss Wallenstein and to hand over his army to Tilly, the general of the Catholic League. Even at this price he was unable to obtain his son's election, which Richelieu had instructed his envoys to oppose.

The emperor, deprived of his German army and his greatest general, was no longer able to continue the war in Italy. The Catholic princes had always been opposed to the war, and they were eager to bring about peace with France, which they had learnt to regard as

4381*

their ally. On October 13 Father Joseph and his colleague signed the treaty of Ratisbon, which was to
settle the question of the Mantuan succession. The
dukes of Savoy and Guastalla were to receive compensation for the resignation of their claims ; the emperor
was to give formal investiture to the duke of Mantua
within six weeks, and a fortnight after the investiture
had been granted the Imperialists were to quit Mantua,
the Spaniards Montferrat, and the French their conquests in Savoy and Piedmont. After all this had
been done the emperor was to withdraw his forces from
the Grison passes and to destroy the newly-erected
fortifications. France pledged herself to give no assistance, direct or indirect, to the enemies of the emperor.
Copies of the treaty were at once despatched to the
court at Lyons and to the French camp in Italy.

It is extremely improbable that Father Joseph acted
in this matter in opposition to Richelieu's instructions,
and it is certain that he never forfeited the cardinal's
favour or confidence. But Richelieu clamoured that
the envoys had exceeded their powers, and that the
treaty was so disadvantageous to France that it could
not possibly be confirmed. The solution of the problem
seems to be that Father Joseph was playing a preconcerted part at Ratisbon. At all costs he was to
conciliate the Catholic electors to France and to prevent
the election of a king of the Romans. These ends he
could only obtain by signing the treaty. But Richelieu
had so worded the instructions of his representatives
as to reserve to himself the power of rejecting the
terms which they had found it advisable to accept.
And it is possible that events at home made the prompt

Lincoln Christian College

conclusion of peace at this moment peculiarly unaccept-
able to him. The health of Louis XIII. had suffered
from the hot weather in Savoy. The solicitations of
his mother induced him to return to Lyons, and there
he was seized with an attack of dysentery, which was
aggravated by the exhausting treatment then in vogue.
As his doctor bled him seven times in a week, and
administered an innumerable variety of drugs, it is no
wonder that his life was despaired of. The crisis to
which Richelieu must often have looked forward seemed
to have arrived on September 20, when the king
received extreme unction and took a formal farewell of
the world. Gaston of Orleans prepared to succeed to
his brother's crown, if not, as some say, to his brother's
wife. The enemies of the cardinal discussed who
should take his place, and whether it was better to
remove him by imprisonment or by death. Their
schemes were suddenly disconcerted by the king's
recovery; but in the exhaustion of convalescence he
gave way to the incessant pressure of his wife and his
mother, and held out hopes that he would dismiss the
cardinal as soon as peace was concluded. The king's
promise was not very definite; but the mere suspicion
of such an intention was enough to make Richelieu
insist upon the defects of the treaty of Ratisbon.

Meanwhile the news of this treaty reached the French
camp just as the army was advancing to effect the relief
of Casale before October 30. Montmorency had been
recalled to France, and his place was taken by Louis
Marillac, brother of the keeper of the seals, who had
previously commanded the army of Champagne. He
wished to accept the terms, but his colleagues, Schomberg

and d'Effiat, insisted that they were too favourable to
the enemy.   By the truce of Rivalta the Spaniards were
to quit Casale as soon as the citadel had been relieved,
whereas by the treaty they would be allowed to remain
there for two months.   The march was resumed, and on
October 27 the two armies were on the point of an
engagement, when Mazarin appeared between them
at the imminent risk of being shot for his pains, and
announced that peace had been arranged.   The Spaniards
agreed to quit Montferrat at once, on condition that
Casale was handed over to the duke of Maine, the son
of the duke of Mantua, who was to pledge himself to
maintain only a native garrison in the citadel.   The
French had so far triumphed that Casale had never been
taken, and that they retained their conquests in Savoy
and Piedmont as security for the evacuation by the
Imperialists of Mantua and the Valtelline.

The news of the relief of Casale reached the French
court as it was returning from Lyons to Paris after the
king's recovery, and Mary de Medici had a bonfire
kindled to celebrate the event.   She believed that the
Italian difficulty was at an end, and that Louis would
now dismiss the hated minister, whom he no longer
needed.   To her astonishment the king opposed an
obstinate resistance to her entreaties, refused to recognise any engagements made during his illness, and
desired his mother to abandon her ill-founded enmity
against the cardinal.   At last Mary's passion got the
better of the crafty dissimulation which was the tradition
of her family.   On November 10 she picked a violent
quarrel, in the king's presence, with Madame de Combalet, the cardinal's favourite niece.   After upbraiding

her in language that would· have disgraced a fishwife,
she bade her leave her service and presence for ever.
The king himself escorted the young woman, weeping
and scared by such an unexpected scene, to the door,
which was soon afterwards entered by the uncle. Mary
de Medici turned her fury upon him with the same
vehemence of language and gesticulation. Richelieu
made no attempt to defend himself, but listened in
respectful silence, and quitted the room. Then the
queen turned to her son : she accused the cardinal of
designing to marry his niece to the count of Soissons,
to depose Louis, and to place the count on the throne.

Forgetting that she supplied evidence of a preconcerted conspiracy, she divulged her schemes for the
conduct of the government after Richelieu's fall. Michel
Marillac was to become chief minister, and his brother
was to assume the supreme command of the army. The
king made no attempt to interrupt or reply to this
violent monologue. He retired to his chamber and
threw himself in a rage upon his bed. He was unwilling
to quarrel irretrievably with his mother, but he had no
intention of parting with his minister. The very com-
plaints which he had listened to only furnished a striking proof of Richelieu's fidelity. The basis of the
queen-mother's resentment was that the cardinal was
more devoted to the king than to herself. Louis's
chamberlain and favourite, St. Simon, father of the
famous memoir-writer, strengthened his resolution by
urging that he had duties not only as a son, but also
as a king, and that the cardinal was necessary to France.
To escape any further maternal intimidation, the king
determined to depart for Versailles.

Meanwhile Mary de Medici had convinced herself that her son's silence implied acquiescence. The news of her victory was circulated through Paris, and couriers were sent to announce the cardinal's downfall to foreign courts. The French courtiers crowded to the queen-mother's magnificent palace, the Luxemburg, to offer their congratulations. The rumour spread that Richelieu was collecting his papers and valuables, and was preparing to depart from Paris, if not from France. And it is true that the cardinal was profoundly discouraged. He knew how a violent woman may influence, in spite of himself, a man who dislikes to have troubles and displeasure around him. He may well have feared that Mary de Medici's estimate of her success was no exaggeration. While he thus desponded and hesitated as to his future course, a messenger arrived to bid him join the king at Versailles. Louis had never really doubted as to his ultimate decision; he was conscious that his reign owed its success and its reputation to the cardinal; and if he had to choose between his mother and his minister, his mind was already made up. He only waited till he was safe from interference to announce his determination. On the next day Michel Marillac was called upon to surrender the great seals, and a courier was despatched to Schomberg ordering him to arrest Marshal Marillac and to send him a prisoner to France. November 11, 1630, has come down to history as the "day of dupes."

Richelieu's position was all the stronger for the failure of the attack upon him. Mary de Medici was compelled to acknowledge her defeat, and in December she controlled her rage so far as to be formally recon-

ciled with the cardinal, and to resume her seat in the
council. But she had no intention of abandoning her
desire for vengeance on the man who had thwarted and
humiliated her. As open violence had failed, she determined to try once more the paths of intrigue. Her
elder son had escaped from her influence, but she still
had some control over his younger brother. Gaston's
importance as heir-apparent to the throne was far
greater than his own abilities would have given him,
and he was readily induced to fall in with his mother's
wishes. In January 1631 he appeared in the cardinal's
chamber and openly renounced his friendship; directly
afterwards he set out for Orleans. It was the intention
of the queen-mother to rally round her second son all
the elements of opposition to the monarchy, and, if
necessary, to trust to the chances of a civil war.
Richelieu fully appreciated her designs. To allow her
to remain in impunity at court would only strengthen
and encourage her faction, and the king was easily persuaded to separate himself from an influence which he
now dreaded and disliked. The court journeyed to
Compiègne, and the queen-mother followed to watch
her son. Early in the morning of February 23 the
king and the cardinal hurried back to Paris. Anne of
Austria was ordered to follow her husband, but was
allowed to take a tender farewell of her mother-in-law,
with whom she had been closely united of late years by
common antipathy to Richelieu. They never met again.
Mary de Medici received written instructions to retire
for a time to Moulins, as circumstances made her
presence at court undesirable. The princess of Conti
and other ladies of her household were exiled to their

estates, and Marshal Bassompierre, an ally of the Marillacs, was committed to a prison from which he never emerged while Richelieu lived.

The cardinal now tried to conciliate Gaston, but the prince was persuaded by his followers to reject all offers, and in March he retired for a second time to Lorraine. Meanwhile Mary de Medici obstinately refused to leave Compiègne, and endeavoured to excite sympathy by representing that she was harshly imprisoned by the man whom she had raised to greatness. Her residence so near to Paris was a constant source of annoyance to the king and minister, but they did not venture to risk unpopularity by removing her by force. Their end was at last effected by relaxing the careful watch hitherto maintained over her movements. Weary of inaction, the queen escaped from France in July, and made her way to Brussels. She was destined never to revisit the country in which her marriage had enabled her to play so prominent a part.

These exciting events had distracted public attention from the Mantuan question, which had so long absorbed it. Hostilities had been terminated by the truce concluded by Mazarin before Casale, but as Richelieu had steadily refused to confirm the treaty of Ratisbon, no permanent settlement had been agreed to. Early in 1631 the French envoys, Toiras and Servien, proceeded to Cherasco in Piedmont to meet the plenipotentiaries of the emperor, and the representatives of Spain, Savoy, and Mantua. The chief difficulties arose about the compensation to be given to the duke of Savoy for the resignation of his claims, and about the dates at which the various powers were to abandon their conquests.

At length everything was settled by two treaties, in April and June, and in July the duke of Nevers received the imperial investiture of Mantua and Montferrat. To the surprise of contemporaries, it was the duke of Mantua who had most reason to be dissatisfied with the treaties of Cherasco. His champion, France, compelled him to sell the greater part of Montferrat to the duke of Savoy. The explanation was not long a secret. Richelieu publicly agreed to restore Pinerolo in order to satisfy European opinion and to obtain peace. But he was determined to keep the fortress if any opportunity offered. Victor Amadeus, instructed by the failure of his father's policy, was inclined to the French alliance which his marriages rendered natural. The offer of larger territories in Montferrat induced him to consent that the French should have Pinerolo, and a secret treaty to that effect was signed on March 31. The only difficulty that remained was to obtain some plausible pretext for breaking the treaty of Cherasco, which stipulated for the restoration of all French conquests. Richelieu was not at a loss for an expedient. He complained that Spain kept so large a garrison in Milan as to excite the fear of a new attack on Mantua, and he called upon Savoy to give surety against any new league with the Spaniards. Victor Amadeus, after feigning an appeal for aid to Milan, agreed that Pinerolo should be handed over as a pledge, nominally to the Swiss, but in reality to the French. In 1632 this flimsy pretence was abandoned, and Pinerolo was bought by France.

Thus Richelieu had achieved a complete triumph in these years. He had obtained the submission of the Huguenots; he had defeated the intrigues and the open assaults of his domestic enemies ; he had humbled Spain and the empire ; and he had secured French influence in Italy by seating a Frenchman in the duchy of Mantua, and by obtaining for France the key of the Alpine passes.

CHAPTER VI

FRANCE INVOLVED IN THE EUROPEAN WAR

1631–1635

Richelieu made duke and peer—Threatened coalition in favour of Gaston—Lorraine—Treaty of Vic—Gaston's marriage and retreat to Brussels—Gustavus Adolphus in Germany—Services which he renders to France—Louis XIII. and Richelieu in Lorraine—Treaty of Liverdun—Gaston in France—Montmorency—Battle of Castelnaudari—Execution of Montmorency—Gaston retires to Brussels—Death of Gustavus Adolphus—Illness and recovery of Richelieu—Fall and imprisonment of Châteauneuf—Richelieu and his colleagues—League of Heilbronn—Renewed invasion of Lorraine—Surrender of Nancy—Abdication of Charles IV.—Complete occupation of Lorraine—Gaston's marriage with Margaret annulled—Return of Gaston and Puylaurens—Imprisonment and death of Puylaurens—Wallenstein's policy—His death—Battle of Nordlingen—Break up of the Protestant League in Germany—Treaty of Prague—Dangers to France if the war came to an end—Seizure of the elector of Trier by the Spaniards—France declares war against Spain.

LOUIS XIII. was not ungrateful to the minister who in seven years had already done enough to make the reign notable in the history of France. In August 1631 he issued letters-patent creating Richelieu duke and peer. On September 5 the ceremony took place of admitting the new peer to the parliament. Condé, Montmorency, and the chief nobles of France formed his escort, but such a crowd had assembled at the doors that the procession could only make its way to the grand chamber through the galleries. Richelieu was never popular, but the people appreciated the grandeur of his aims and his achievements. They admired, if they did not love. At the same time the cardinal received the government of Brittany, so important for his maritime and commercial projects. Nor was it at home only that his merits were applauded. The Republic of Venice, always eager to recognise greatness outside her own walls, sent a special envoy to offer him the rank of noble, with power to name any of his relatives as his successor.

But no one knew better than Richelieu that he was only on the threshold of greater difficulties than those which he had already overcome. The triumph of French policy in Italy had provoked and alarmed the house of Hapsburg. Both Austria and Spain were now fully alive to the danger which threatened them if France, united at home, were to espouse the cause of their enemies in Germany and the United Provinces. Such a catastrophe could only be prevented by doing all in their power to revive the embers of dissension in France. Spain was the more immediately interested in this because the line of provinces through which a connection was maintained between Lombardy and the Netherlands ran along the eastern frontier of France. If the emperor could only crush the opposition in Germany, Spain would be free to suppress its dangerous rival in the west, and the means for attaining this end were sufficiently obvious. The heir to the French crown was more dangerous outside France than he could be within. With the assistance of foreign troops, and the support of the dis-contented nobles and parliaments of his own country, Gaston might succeed in overthrowing the minister whom his favourites had taught him to detest. And with the fall of Richelieu France might again become as powerless and contemptible as it had been under the regency of Mary de Medici.

The headquarters of the conspiracy were at Nancy, where Gaston had taken refuge. Charles IV. of Lorraine was eager to free his duchy from the control which France had secured by the seizure in 1552 of the three bishoprics of Metz, Toul, and Verdun. He had already raised an army of 15,000 men, and he had persuaded the emperor to enforce his suzerainty over the three bishoprics by the capture of Moyenvic, a disputed de-pendency. With the assistance of troops from the Netherlands and from Germany, Lorraine might be a formidable starting-point for an invasion of France. Gaston was to be bound to the confederacy by a mar-riage with the duke's sister, Margaret.

But Richelieu was far too prompt to allow his enemies to complete their preparations. In the winter of 1631 he despatched la Force and Schomberg to drive the Imperialists from Moyenvic, while he carried off the king and court to Metz, leaving Soissons as lieutenant-governor in Paris. Complete success rewarded both movements, Moyenvic was taken, and the duke of Lorraine hastened to conclude the Treaty of Vic (January 6, 1632), by which he promised to withdraw from all hostile alliances, and to expel from his territories all the enemies of France. Richelieu hoped by depriving Gaston of his refuge to induce him to

accept a reconciliation, but the latter was persuaded
by his chief adviser, Puylaurens, to withdraw to Brussels.
The plot was postponed and not abandoned. Charles IV.
had no intention of observing the promises, and almost
at the moment of the conclusion of the treaty of Vic
Gaston was secretly married to Margaret of Lorraine.

While Richelieu was engaged in averting the immediate perils which threatened France, events were
occurring in Germany which were destined not only to
frustrate the schemes of his enemies, but to open the
way for a new policy of aggrandisement and annexation.
In 1632 the cardinal began to dream of that extension
of the French frontier to the Rhine which becomes so
dominant a tradition in subsequent generations. The
beginning of this great enterprise was one of the many
important results of the victories of Gustavus Adolphus.
Although the Swedish king had been urged by Richelieu
to invade Germany, and although a formal treaty between them was concluded at Bärwalde in January
1631, the aims of the two great protagonists were far
from harmonious. For the chief objects of Gustavus,
the aggrandisement of Sweden and the maintenance or
extension of Protestantism, Richelieu cared not at all. To
him the Swedish army was merely a tool to be used for
the humiliation of the house of Hapsburg, and to divert
the attention of Austria from Italy and France. He
would have preferred to attain his ends by an alliance
with the Catholic League, if that had been possible, and
it was only when he found that Maximilian of Bavaria
had too many interests in common with the emperor
that he finally decided on a treaty with Sweden. And
his diplomacy, skilful as it was, was insufficient to keep

a man like Gustavus Adolphus in the leading-strings of
France.   The latter set himself to secure his position
in the north before he would risk a direct attack upon
the enemies whom he had come to seek.   The emperor's
obstinate persistence in enforcing the Edict of Restitution
drove the Lutheran princes into an alliance with Sweden.
The hesitation of John George of Saxony, averse to the
intervention of a foreigner in German affairs, and still
more unwilling to acknowledge a superior, was finally
overcome by the sack of Magdeburg.   Having at last
achieved his first aim, Gustavus Adolphus advanced to
meet the army of the League under Tilly.   Few more
important battles have been fought than that of Leipzig
(September 7, 1631).   On its issue were staked the maintenance of Protestantism in Germany, the very existence
of Sweden as a state, and in a lesser degree the future
of France and its great minister.   If Tilly had
triumphed, it would have been immensely difficult to
resist the foreign coalition in favour of Gaston of
Orleans.

The victory of Gustavus Adolphus removed this
danger, but the attention of Europe was at once concentrated upon the conqueror's future movements.   If
he marched straight upon Vienna, it seemed impossible
that the emperor, without either army or general, could
make any effective resistance, and terms of peace might
be dictated in the capital of the Austrian Hapsburgs.
This seemed the most obvious policy, and it had
much to recommend it to Richelieu, who had always
desired to employ the Swedes against Austria and to
spare the Catholic League.   But Gustavus Adolphus
was jealous of French dictation, and resolute to follow

his own course. Leaving John George to invade
Bohemia, he led his own army against the defenceless
states of the Rhine prelates. No resistance was offered
to his triumphal march, and before the end of the year
Mainz itself was in his hands. That Richelieu was
chagrined by his decision is undeniable. In his *Memoirs*
he asserts that Gustavus Adolphus, like Hannibal, knew
how to conquer, but not how to use his victory.

But in spite of the cardinal's criticism it is doubtful
whether France could have been better served by a
direct attack upon Vienna than she was by Gustavus's
triumphal march along the "priests' lane." The
European coalition in favour of Gaston, which depended
more upon Spain than upon Austria, was practically annihilated. The duke of Lorraine was deprived of the
allies who might have interfered to protect him from
the consequences of his continued intrigues, and of his
treacherous breach of the treaty of Vic. But the chief
result was to give an opening for French intervention
in Southern Germany. The ecclesiastical electors
hastened to implore the mediation of the cardinal, and
the archbishop of Trier promptly placed himself under
French protection, and offered to admit French garrisons
into his fortresses of Hermanstein (now Ehrenbreitstein)
and Philipsburg. The marquis de Brézé, Richelieu's
brother-in-law, was sent to warn Gustavus Adolphus
from a further advance into Elsass, and to negotiate
terms for the neutrality of Bavaria and Cologne.

In order to profit by the opportunity which the
Swedish successes offered to him, Richelieu determined
to make himself master of Lorraine, an enterprise for
which the conduct of Charles IV. offered a convenient

pretext. Gaston, after collecting troops in Brussels, had returned to Lorraine on his way to France, where his emissaries were active in stirring up the malcontent nobles to active measures against the cardinal. As a warning to his enemies, Richelieu brought Marshal Marillac to trial for peculation before a special commission, and he was condemned and executed (May 8). Richelieu then recalled the French army, which had already appeared on the Rhine and occupied Ehrenbreitstein, and carried the king with him to Lorraine. In eight days the campaign was over. The capture of Pont-à-Mousson, and the advance of Marshal d'Effiat to lay siege to Nancy, brought the duke to his knees. By the treaty of Liverdun (June 26) he undertook to observe the promises he had made at Vic, to do homage for his duchy of Bar, and to sell the county of Clermont to France. As security for his good faith he was to leave his brother, the cardinal of Lorraine, as a hostage, and to place the fortresses of Stenay and Jametz in French hands. The French army was now free to renew the campaign in Germany, and in spite of the discouragement caused by the death of d'Effiat, his successor, d'Estrées, succeeded in driving the Spaniards from the city of Trier. By thus seizing the bridge over the Moselle, the French cut off the most direct route between the Netherlands and the Spanish provinces in Italy.

Having drawn the teeth of the duke of Lorraine, it was now high time for Richelieu to turn his attention to Gaston, who had entered France on June 8, and had issued a manifesto containing a violent attack upon the cardinal. Personally the heir to the throne was a

contemptible antagonist, but he had succeeded in gaining
over the greatest noble in France, after the princes of
the royal blood.   Henri de Montmorency, the last bearer
of a famous name in history, had won reputation as a
soldier at Avigliana, and had since been on terms of
affectionate intimacy with Richelieu, who relied on his
fidelity.   But the young duke was discontented with
the humble part which the great nobles had to play
under the cardinal's rule.   He coveted his ancestors'
office of constable, which had been suppressed, and he
resented the harsh treatment of his province of Languedoc.   Above all, the influence of his wife, a relative of
Mary de Medici, urged him to come forward as the
champion of the oppressed mother and brother of the
king.   He invited Gaston to advance from Burgundy
into Languedoc, and it was confidently hoped that his
name and reputation would give the rebels a firm footing in Southern France.   But Richelieu was now to
reap the reward of his firm and prudent policy.   The
Huguenots, contented with religious toleration, refused
to join a movement which was encouraged by Spain.
The chief nobles and governors of provinces, warned by
the fate of Marillac, hesitated to commit themselves
until some substantial success had been obtained, and
the leaders of the rising were at variance among themselves.   Puylaurens, eager to maintain his ascendency
over the feeble Gaston, was jealous of Montmorency's
influence, and the latter's claim to command was disputed by d'Elbœuf.   These dissensions had already
assured the failure of the rebels when they came into
collision with the royal army under Schomberg at
Castelnaudari (September 1).   A chivalrous but reckless

cavalry charge carried Montmorency into the middle of
the enemy ; his horse was killed under him, and he was
carried from the field wounded and a prisoner.

Gaston, who accepted the devotion of his adherents
without sharing their risks, and who had taken no
part in the battle, at once realised that all was lost, and
opened negotiations with Louis. There was no dis-
position to treat him harshly, and he received most
lenient terms from his brother. On condition of abandoning all hostile alliances, he recovered all his appanages,
and an amnesty was promised to most of his adherents,
with the significant exception of Montmorency. Richelieu
knew how to be moderate in the hour of victory. The
king presided in person at a meeting of the estates of
Languedoc at Béziers, and restored for a money payment
the liberties of which the province had been deprived
in 1629.

Attention was now concentrated upon the fate of
Montmorency, who had been basely deserted by his
accomplices, but whose life was pleaded for by illustrious
relatives, and even by crowned heads. Richelieu, however, merciful as he had been to the mass of the rebels,
was determined to make an example of their leader.
He would teach the French nobles that rebellion, even
in the interests of the heir to the throne, was not an
enterprise to be lightly undertaken. To the king he
urged that Montmorency's execution was the only way
to make Gaston powerless by depriving him of adherents.
A still more potent argument to himself was to be found
in a remark made by Bullion, and which is reproduced
by the cardinal himself—that the house of Montmorency
was so powerful in Languedoc that the people regarded

the royal power as imaginary.   To Richelieu, the duke's
removal may well have seemed an almost necessary step
to that absorption of the provinces under a powerful
monarchy and a centralised administration which was
the grand object of his life.   In his *Memoirs* he pleads,
not without plausibility, that his severity proved his
devotion to France at the expense of his own personal
interests.   To have spared the prisoner would have been
an easy method of gaining popularity.   To punish him
was to expose his own life to the risk of assassination,
because it would convince his enemies that they could
only secure themselves by his death.   But these considerations had little weight with Richelieu, who was
superior to vulgar terrors, and who had assimilated, either
consciously or unconsciously, the maxim of Machiavelli,
that it is safer to be feared than to be loved.   Montmorency was brought to trial before the parliament of
Toulouse, whose competence to pass judgment on a peer
was more than doubtful, condemned to death, and
executed on the same day (October 30).   Men to whom
the traditions of the civil wars were still familiar, and
who remembered the impunity with which princes and
nobles conspired under the regency, must have realised
that a new era had begun for France when a minister
of the crown ventured to bring to the scaffold the last
male of a family whose name was so honourably and
conspicuously written in the country's history.

One result of the execution Richelieu had probably
failed to foresee.   Although Gaston had omitted to
stipulate for Montmorency's pardon, even his torpid
selfishness could not but feel the ignominy which the
fate of his chivalrous supporter threw upon himself.

His own fears and those of Puylaurens were kindled by the recollection that his marriage with Margaret of Lorraine had not yet been acknowledged, and that it would never be tolerated by the king and cardinal. On November 6 he fled from Tours, and again sought refuge in Brussels.

Thus the heir to the throne was once more in the hands of the enemies of France, and the task of depriving them of this dangerous weapon had to be commenced afresh. At the same time an event occurred in Germany which altered the whole aspect of affairs in Europe, and demanded the exercise of all Richelieu's prudent watchfulness. Gustavus Adolphus had listened to French remonstrances so far as to abstain from advancing into Elsass and to respect the neutrality of Trier. But he refused to resign the ecclesiastical territories which he had already seized, and the attempt to arrange terms with the leaders of the Catholic League proved a failure. Early in 1632 the Swedes advanced against Bavaria, and Tilly was defeated and slain in attempting to dispute the passage of the Lech. Gustavus Adolphus entered Munich in triumph, and Maximilian was driven from his own duchy. Austria was once more exposed to invasion, and the army of the League was no longer able to defend the emperor. In his despair Ferdinand II. had been compelled to appeal to Wallenstein, who recovered his command on terms which made him an independent potentate. With an army which was brought together by the magic of his reputation, and which he treated as his private following, Wallenstein had already driven the Saxons from Bohemia, and he now advanced to check the eastward march of the

Swedes.   At Nürnberg Gustavus Adolphus met with
his first check, as he dared not attack the enemy's
intrenchments, and failed to force him into a pitched
battle.   From Nürnberg Wallenstein drew the Swedes
after him into Saxony, and on November 16 their
heroic king lost his life on the glorious field of Lützen.

At this very moment Richelieu was lying on a bed
of sickness, from which it seemed more than possible
that he would never rise again.   After settling affairs
in Languedoc, Louis XIII. had hurried back to Paris,
while the cardinal undertook to escort the queen on a
tour through Western France, where she was to visit his
home at Richelieu and his great conquest, La Rochelle.
But an internal abscess had long preyed upon a frame
that had never been strong, and to this disorder was
now added disease of the bladder.   The cardinal was
compelled to stop at Bordeaux, and to leave the task of
entertaining Anne of Austria to his uncle, the commander
de la Porte.   About November 20 his condition seemed
almost hopeless, and in Paris the rumour spread that he
was dead.   Open enemies and faithless friends exulted
over the expected removal of an oppressor or a too-
powerful patron.   Châteauneuf, the keeper of the seals,
who owed his elevation to Richelieu, was indiscreet
enough to betray his hopes of succeeding to the position
of his dying colleague.   But an indomitable spirit often
triumphs over the weakness of its mortal covering.
Richelieu recovered as if by a miracle, and as soon
as he had rejoined the court he hastened to punish
those personal affronts which in his eyes were almost
as unpardonable as serious crimes against the state.
Châteauneuf was accused, on the loose assertions of the

cardinal's spies, of being engaged in an intrigue with the duchess of Chevreuse, the queen-mother, and Henrietta Maria of England. His real offence was that he had deserted Richelieu at Bordeaux, that he had danced before the queen while his patron was thought to be dying, and that he had allowed himself to dream of succeeding to the office of first minister. For this he was deprived of the seals and imprisoned at Angoulême, but the fact that he was never brought to trial goes far to prove that there was little foundation for the graver charges against him.

Richelieu's recovery was exceedingly opportune, as he found France threatened by three simultaneous dangers. The death of Gustavus Adolphus weakened the league against the Austrian Hapsburgs, and might easily lead to its dissolution. The United Provinces were negotiating for a truce with Spain, and if this were arranged, the Spaniards would be free to carry out their schemes for assisting Gaston, who had again joined the enemies of his country. Never did the cardinal display more coolness and decision than at this crisis, when the whole weight of affairs rested on his own shoulders. His colleagues in the council, of whom the chief were Bullion and Bouthillier, had one great qualification—devotion to their chief. They were always consulted by him, but the decision he always reserved to himself, and they were quite content to carry out a policy which they knew themselves to be incapable of originating. The only personage who may have possessed influence over Richelieu was Father Joseph, who was not officially a member of the council, and whose relations with the cardinal have always been something of an enigma to

historians. Such evidence as we possess, however, goes
to prove that the influence of the "grey cardinal" has
been exaggerated by Richelieu's detractors, and that the
special subjects on which he was consulted were affairs
in Germany and the relations with Rome. Louis XIII.
himself, whose penetration and decision the cardinal is
never tired of contrasting with his own "simplicity,"
was conspicuously devoid of the qualities which his
minister attributes to him. His notes on the minutes
of the council, which are published in the great collection
of M. d'Avenel, proved that he never dreamed of disput-
ing the conclusions of an adviser whose superiority he
always recognised even when he was most inclined to
resent it.

Early in 1633 two of the ablest of French diplom-
atists, Feuquières and Charnacé, were despatched to
Germany and Holland, and their instructions, which are
model state-papers, show how clearly Richelieu compre-
hended the situation, and how he planned to turn it to
the advantage of France. While avoiding as long as
possible an open declaration of war, he wished to
strengthen all the elements of opposition to the house
of Hapsburg, and to seize every opportunity for strengthening the monarchy at home and for extending the
power of France on the eastern frontier. In Germany
the embassy of Feuquières was completely successful.
The alliance of France with Sweden, which was now
governed by Oxenstiern on behalf of Christina, the young
daughter of Gustavus, was renewed. At Heilbronn the
influence of the French envoy was mainly instrumental
in securing the confirmation of the Protestant League,
which was strengthened by further additions at the later

conference at Frankfurt. French diplomacy defeated the attempt of John George of Saxony to procure the direction of the League, which was given to Oxenstiern, but, to his great disgust, with strictly limited powers. Richelieu had regarded the death of Gustavus with composure, if not with secret complacency, and events justified his view. The Swedish king was an unmanageable ally, and continued successes might have enabled him to found a power independent of, and possibly formidable to, France. His removal rendered the Swedes again dependent upon French support, and at the same time enabled French influence gradually to supplant that of Sweden in Germany.

In Holland Charnacé was equally successful. By making dexterous use of the divisions among the seven provinces he succeeded in frustrating the negotiations with the Netherlands, where the Spanish power suffered a severe blow by the death of the popular and prudent infanta, Clara Isabella. The continuance of the Dutch war prevented the Spaniards from sending assistance to Charles IV. of Lorraine, who had been encouraged by the death of the Swedish king to disregard the obligations he had contracted at Liverdun. This gave Richelieu the opportunity which he wanted for the annexation of a province whose possession would be as advantageous as its hostility was dangerous to France. He had already employed the labours of learned antiquarians to prove that the imperial suzerainty was a usurpation which no lapse of time could legalise, and that Lorraine was properly a dependency of the French crown. Fortified with their arguments, he proceeded to take active measures. On the ground that the

stipulated homage had never been paid for Bar, the
parliament of Paris declared the duchy confiscated.
Saint Chaumont was sent with an army to advance
upon Nancy, and in August Richelieu set out with the
king to direct operations on the spot.   Charles IV.,
as unprepared as ever to resist invasion, sent his brother,
the cardinal of Lorraine, to offer to annul the marriage
between Gaston and Margaret, and to propose on his
own behalf a marriage with Madame de Combalet.
Richelieu refused the proffered honour to his niece,
and demanded that Nancy should be surrendered as
a pledge of the duke's good faith.   As this condition
was rejected as too harsh, the French laid siege to the
capital of Lorraine, which was regarded as one of the
best fortresses of Europe.   Charles IV. now gave way,
and agreed to surrender Nancy, but he still hoped for
the arrival of Spanish troops from Italy, and ordered
the commander of the citadel to delay the formal cession.
But the duke of Feria, who had already marched from
Milan through the Valtelline, was delayed at Constance
by the Swedes under count Horn.   This check deprived
Charles of his last hope, and on September 25 Richelieu
accompanied Louis in his formal entry into Nancy.   He
was provided beforehand with an excuse for retaining
a pledge which he had no intention of relinquishing.
During the siege the Princess Margaret, with the con-
nivance of her brothers, had escaped from the city to
Luxemburg, whence she proceeded to join her husband in
Brussels.   Earlier in the year the creation of a parliament
at Metz had cut off the last link between the three
bishoprics and the empire.   The lilies supplanted the
imperial eagle, and the duchy of Lorraine, with all its

chief fortresses garrisoned by French troops, was practically a province of France. It was in vain that Charles IV. sought to disarm the enmity of Louis by abdicating in favour of his brother, who resigned the cardinalate and married his cousin Claude. France refused to recognise the marriage, and the new duke and his bride found themselves compelled to escape imprisonment by flying to Florence. Their departure enabled Richelieu to complete the occupation of Lorraine by seizing the last fortresses and by establishing a *conseil souverain* at Nancy for the administration of justice.

Although Margaret of Lorraine had escaped, Richelieu could now proceed at leisure to procure the dissolution of her marriage with Gaston. This union he had always regarded with such aversion that contemporaries attributed it to the desire to marry his niece to the heir of the French throne. At first it was decided to appeal to the pope for a divorce, but Urban VIII. insisted upon trying the case at Rome, and Richelieu dreaded delay and Spanish influence. Accordingly a civil suit was instituted before the parliament of Paris under the absurd form of a charge of abduction against the duke of Lorraine. The decision of the court was pronounced on September 5, 1634. The marriage was declared to have been invalidly contracted, and Charles IV. was found guilty of treason. To appease the pope an envoy was sent to Rome to explain that the decision did not affect the ecclesiastical aspect of the marriage, and that there was no intention to contest the papal jurisdiction.

About this time Mary de Medici, weary of her exile

in Brussels, and jealous of Puylaurens, who would allow
her no influence over her second son, made overtures
for a reconciliation with the king and cardinal. But
Richelieu would have nothing to do with his former
patroness, and had little difficulty in inducing Louis
XIII. to fix impossible conditions as the price of his
mother's return. At the same time he was as anxious
as ever for a reconciliation with Gaston, whose return
was almost necessary to secure the unity of France in
the face of foreign enemies. Negotiations were being
carried on with Brussels when the capture of one of
the prince's agents revealed the actual conclusion of a
treaty with Spain for the invasion of France. This
discovery exasperated the cardinal, and he openly
declared to the king in council that there were only
two means of foiling his brother's intrigues. The one
was the birth of a son, which depended upon the grace
of God, and the other was the altering of the succession,
which involved a revolution in the fundamental laws
and traditions of France. The dangers of the latter
alternative would not have deterred Richelieu from
urging its adoption, but it was rendered unnecessary
by Gaston's submission. The complete conquest of
Lorraine and the active measures which were taken to
annul the marriage terrified Gaston and Puylaurens,
who had both discovered that the Spaniards only used
them as tools for their own ends. A golden bridge
was built for the return of the baffled conspirators.
Gaston recovered his appanages, with the government of
Auvergne instead of Orleans, while Puylaurens, together
with the rank of duke and peer, received the hand of a
wealthy heiress. But it was soon evident that their

acceptance of these terms involved only a partial
reconciliation.   To the arguments of an ecclesiastical
deputation, which tried to convince him of the nullity
of his marriage, Gaston lent a polite but evasive attention.   It was discovered that he had written to Rome
to protest beforehand against the validity of any acts
or admissions that might be extorted from him after his
return to France.   This obstinacy Richelieu attributed
to the continued intrigues of Puylaurens, who had
indiscreetly boasted that if anything happened to Louis
XIII. he would be first minister under his successor.
He had to learn that it was safer to plot in Brussels
than in Paris, and that his marriage with a relative of
the cardinal was not enough to secure his impunity.
In February 1635 he was suddenly seized and imprisoned
at Vincennes, where a natural death saved him from
the penalties of treason.   Deprived of his chief adviser
and absorbed in sensual pleasures, Gaston fell for a
time into insignificance, and was compelled to accept
the divorce from Margaret, which was ultimately pronounced by a synod of Gallican clergy.

All this time the Swedes, in spite of their king's
death and the vacillation of the elector of Saxony, had
been more than holding their own in Germany, while
French influence was steadily extended in the south-
west.   In 1633 the elector of Cologne had formally
put his estates under French protection, and the duke
of Wurtemberg, unable to defend Montbéliard against
the Spaniards, handed over both town and citadel to a
French garrison.   In the next year several towns in
Elsass also threw their gates open to the French, who
thus acquired their first footing in a province which

was destined to be Richelieu's chief territorial gift to
his country.

The chief cause of these successes, and of the failure
of the imperial forces to profit by the death of
Gustavus Adolphus, was undoubtedly the conduct of
Wallenstein.   The great general had resumed his command with the firm intention of securing, not the
emperor's interests, but his own.   With the religious
objects of Ferdinand II. and the Catholic League he was
entirely out of sympathy.   His object was to make
himself a great prince of the empire, and to use his
military superiority to impose a general pacification
upon the warring sects, so as to prevent Germany from
being torn in pieces to serve the selfish ends of foreign
princes.   For Spain, the close and necessary ally of
the emperor, he had the greatest hatred.   When the
Cardinal Infant, Philip IV.'s brother, applied to him for
4000 cavalry, who were needed to bring his army from
Milan to Germany, he refused.   Instead of vigorously
prosecuting the war, he contented himself with his conquest of Bohemia, where he maintained almost royal
state, and whence he carried on simultaneous negotiations with Sweden, France, and the Protestant princes
of Germany.   Richelieu was willing enough to profit by
Wallenstein's inactivity, but he had the keenness to
detect that antipathy to foreign interference which was
at the bottom of his schemes, and he paid little attention to overtures which could bring no advantage to
France.   But at Vienna it did not need much exercise
of Spanish influence to convince Ferdinand that a
general who presumed to treat with foreign states as an
independent prince could not be tolerated in the im-

perial service. In his contract with his employer, Wallenstein had been careful to provide against a second dismissal, but he could not secure himself against assassination. As long as his army was faithful he was safe. But the fidelity of his officers was tampered with by Spanish gold, and on February 15, 1634, he fell under the dagger of traitors who received his pay.

The death of Wallenstein marks a great turning-point in the history of the Thirty Years' War. His army was induced to accept the command of the young king of Hungary, Ferdinand's eldest son. In June the Cardinal Infant led his long-delayed expedition into Germany, and his troops succeeded in joining those of the emperor. At Nordlingen the united armies inflicted a crushing defeat upon the Swedes under Horn and Bernhard of Saxe-Weimar. For the moment it seemed as if the work of Gustavus Adolphus would be undone by the first failure of his successors. The League of Heilbronn, the product of the joint diplomacy of Richelieu and Oxenstiern, was broken to pieces. John George of Saxony hastened to accept the treaty of Prague (May 1635), by which the Edict of Restitution was revoked, and a compromise was arranged between Catholics and Lutherans. Within a few months these terms were accepted by all the Lutheran princes. As far as Germany was concerned, the Thirty Years' War was at an end. The great questions at issue at its commencement had received a solution which satisfied everybody except the German Calvinists, and they were too few and too powerless to continue hostilities by themselves. But the war had long ceased to be a purely German struggle. In the course of years the

German contest had come to involve in itself all the
rivalries and enmities which agitated Europe: the
quarrels of Sweden and Poland, the jealousy of Denmark against its northern neighbour, the struggle of
Spain to reduce the Dutch into subjection, and, above
all, the enmity between France and Spain, which dated
back to the time of Charles V. It was these foreign
interests that prolonged the war for the next thirteen
years.

The great schemes of Richelieu would have been ruined
if the war had been ended by the treaty of Prague. It
is true that the battle of Nordlingen, by weakening
Sweden, had brought some direct gains to France. The
Swedes, who had seized Philipsburg from the Spaniards,
and had hitherto evaded the French demands for its
surrender, were compelled to abandon the fortress, and
Colmar and other strong places in Elsass endeavoured to
obtain security by the admission of French garrisons.
But these and the earlier acquisitions would have to be
surrendered at a general pacification, and Richelieu had
no intention of surrendering them. Nor was this the
only danger. The termination of the German war
would enormously strengthen Spain. If the Spaniards,
freed from the heavy obligation of supporting Austria,
could reduce the Dutch or make peace with them, they
would then be able to throw all their might into the
recovery of their omnipotence in Italy, or even into a
direct attack upon France. And France would be left
without an efficient ally, as Sweden could render little
service in a struggle with Spain.

To avoid these certain and possible disasters, it was
necessary that the war should be continued; and to

secure its continuation only one expedient remained—
the open intervention of France. For such a step
Richelieu had long been preparing, and it would have
been easy enough to find a pretext for hostilities, even
if Spain had not gone out of her way to provide one.
In March 1635 a Spanish force sallied from Luxemburg, surprised the city of Trier, and carried off the
elector a prisoner to the Netherlands. Richelieu at
once sent to the Cardinal Infant to demand the release
of an ecclesiastical dignitary whose sole offence was his
alliance with France. A refusal was followed by the
appearance of a French herald in Brussels, who, with all
the old formalities, declared war against the king of
Spain. Richelieu had engaged France in the greatest
European struggle in which that country had taken part
since the death of Henry II.

CHAPTER VII

REVERSES AND TRIUMPHS

1635–1640

RICHELIEU had long contemplated the possibility of France being forced to take direct part in the war, and he had made ample preparations, so far as they could be effected by diplomacy. He had failed, it is true, to maintain the alliance between Sweden and the Lutheran princes of Germany, and he had never been able to detach the members of the Catholic League from their union with the emperor. On the other hand, he had arranged an offensive and defensive alliance with the

United Provinces, by which the combined forces of the
two states were to be placed under the command of
Frederick Henry, the stadtholder. He had hopes of a
rising in the Netherlands, where many of the nobles
were discontented with the direct rule of Spain, which
had been re-established on the death of the Infanta.
The neutrality of England was assured by Charles I.'s
resolution to dispense with a parliament, without which
he could not hope to obtain the supplies for a war.
With Oxenstiern, who visited Paris in person for the
purpose, a treaty was concluded by which France and
Sweden pledged themselves to conclude no separate
peace with either Austria or Spain. Richelieu's aptest
pupil in diplomacy, the count d'Avaux, had foiled the
confident attempt of Austria to hamper Sweden by
reviving the old feelings of jealousy on the part of
Poland and Denmark. The truce between Sweden and
Poland, originally concluded by French mediation, was
prolonged for another twenty-five years by the same
agency. In Italy, Richelieu arranged a league with
Savoy, Parma, and Mantua for the partition of the
duchy of Milan, and he had hopes that Urban VIII.,
always jealous of Spanish domination, might be brought
to regard the scheme without disfavour. Finally, the
duke de Rohan, who had been skilfully converted from
a dangerous opponent into a loyal agent, was despatched,
with the approval of the Grisons, to occupy the Valtelline, and thus to prevent assistance being sent from
Germany to the Milanese. If these grand schemes had
all been attended with success, the power of Spain
beyond the limits of the peninsula would have been
almost annihilated.

But the most active and far-seeing diplomacy could create neither a trained and disciplined army, nor competent generals in a country which for the last generation had been engaged in nothing but short outbursts of civil war, varied by an occasional brief expedition to Italy. The numbers of the French forces, amounting in all to 130,000 men, excited the astonishment of Europe, where no equal effort had been made during sixteen years of incessant warfare. But nothing was gained to correspond to these exhausting preparations. The campaign in the Netherlands, to which Richelieu attached the greatest importance, ended in complete failure. The expected rising never took place, as discontent with Spanish rule gave way to patriotic indignation at the outrages of French invaders. The arrival of imperial troops, set free by the treaty of Prague, enabled the Spaniards to raise the siege of Louvain, and Frederick Henry of Orange, who commanded the combined French and Dutch forces, was not strong or enterprising enough to risk a battle in the open field. On the German frontiers the French succeeded in defending their position in Elsass and Lorraine, but their aid was not sufficient to enable Bernhard of Saxe-Weimar to hold his own on the Rhine. By the end of 1635 Frankfort, Mannheim, Heidelberg, and Mainz had fallen into the hands of the Imperialists. In Italy, although Rohan succeeded in occupying the Valtelline, and thus cut off German aid from Lombardy, the attempted invasion of the Milanese proved a fiasco. Victor Amadeus and Créqui, at the head of a large force of Piedmontese and French, wasted the whole summer in a futile siege of Valenza. Meanwhile the

Spaniards enjoyed a complete ascendency at sea, which enabled them to maintain a constant intercourse both with the Netherlands and the Italian peninsula. It was a bitter humiliation for France when a Spanish fleet occupied and garrisoned the two little islands of Lérins, off the coast of Provence.

Richelieu's magnificent schemes of conquest were for the time at an end, and the cardinal himself is not free from some responsibility for his failure. His past experience had taught him to be always suspicious, and he could not trust his generals. He was so long used to command himself, and so confident in his own capacity, that he thought his orders from a distance must be better than those of a mistrusted subordinate on the spot. When possible, he divided the command, so that differences between the two generals might secure his own supremacy. But the chief cause of failure is to be found in the character of the French soldiery. In the course of three generations of civil strife they had lost every military virtue except courage. They could fight in face of the enemy, but in camp they were disorderly, mutinous, impatient alike of hardship and of control. Against veterans trained in the school of Gustavus and of Tilly such troops were worse than useless. But for the support of Bernhard of Saxe-Weimar and his hardy mercenaries the campaign of 1635 would have been still more disastrous.

In spite of the check he had received, Richelieu determined to continue his aggressive policy in 1636. In Italy Victor Amadeus and Créqui advanced to the Ticino, where they inflicted a crushing defeat on the Spanish army. But the duke of Savoy was on bad

terms with his colleague, and prevented any attempt
to join Rohan, who was waiting near Lake Como for a
combined advance upon Milan. In August the troops
returned to winter quarters. Meanwhile a French
army had invaded Franche Comté and laid siege to
Dôle. But the population was better treated, and
therefore more loyal than that of any other Spanish
province, and Dôle was still untaken when the unexpected news arrived that France itself was exposed to a
formidable invasion. Frederick Henry had succeeded
in retaking the fortress of Schenk, which the enemy had
captured in the previous year, and the French troops
in the Netherlands were preparing to relieve Liège,
besieged by the imperial general Piccolomini. But the
arrival of the Bavarian commander, John of Werth, and
of a considerable Spanish force, under the Cardinal
Infant Leopold, encouraged the enemy to attempt a
more ambitious enterprise. Patching up terms with
the Liègeois, the imperial troops marched southwards,
and in July crossed the frontier of Picardy. No
preparations had been made for resistance. The
border fortresses of La Chapelle and Le Câtelet surrendered at the first summons, the passage of the
Somme was forced with ease, and the enemy advanced
burning and ravaging to the banks of the Oise. So
great was the terror inspired by his mounted Croats
that the name of John of Werth served French mothers
for years as a bogey to frighten children with.

Paris was panic-stricken. Louis XIII., always
gloomy, was more reserved than ever. Everybody
seemed to throw the responsibility for danger and
disaster upon the minister who had declared war.

Richelieu alone preserved his courage and presence of mind in a crisis that would have daunted a lesser man. In spite of the entreaties and warnings of his friends, he proceeded almost unattended through the streets to the Hotel de Ville to call upon the citizens to make sacrifices for the safety of their country. The effect of his undaunted resolution and confidence was magical. Paris hastened to respond to his appeal with a devotion like that which was shown a century and a half later in the revolutionary wars. The municipality, the parliament, the Sorbonne, and the trading guilds vied with each other in offering grants of money, and volunteers hastened to enrol their names on the list which was drawn up in the Hotel de Ville. The example of Paris was followed by the other large towns, and the Huguenots were as eager to prove their patriotism as the Catholics. Richelieu had many enemies, but for the moment men thought only of his services to the country.

The danger proved less than it had at first appeared. The invaders succeeded in taking Corbie, but they never advanced beyond the Oise. The Dutch were threatening the Netherlands, and the Cardinal Infant feared to involve his troops too far in the interior of France. By the time that the new levies were ready to take the field, John of Werth was in full retreat towards the frontier. No attempt was made to harass the enemy, and the French army contented itself with undertaking the siege of Corbie, which was forced to open its gates in November. At the same time an attempted invasion of Burgundy by the duke of Lorraine was successfully repulsed. France had failed to make conquests, but within its own frontiers it was still invincible.

But though France was saved, the minister was still exposed to personal danger. The Spaniards had striven to revive internal disunion, and the manifesto of the Cardinal Infant had been filled with denunciations of Richelieu. The duke of Orleans and the count of Soissons, instead of being conciliated by their appointments to command the army of defence, thought only of the opportunity to gratify their personal ambition or their desire for vengeance. Soissons had been irritated by the refusal of the command in Elsass, entrusted to the cardinal de la Valette, and deemed himself insulted by the proposal of a marriage with Richelieu's niece, Madame de Combalet. The two princes, laying aside their former animosity, formed a dangerous conspiracy against the object of their mutual hatred. Their schemes went so far as to project the assassination of the cardinal at Amiens, but Gaston's courage failed him at the moment when he should have given the concerted signal. The failure of the Spanish invasion and the recapture of Corbie discouraged the conspirators, and an attempt to tamper with the fidelity of the troops proved futile. Dreading discovery and arrest, the two princes fled from the army in November, Gaston to Blois and Soissons to Sedan. Negotiations proving futile, the king and cardinal led an army against Blois in January 1637. Gaston was unprepared for resistance, and was allowed to make peace on easy terms. Soissons, more obstinate or more distrustful, held out till July, when he also made his submission, but refused to return to court.

Unfortunately discontent was by no means confined to the princes and great nobles. The middle and lower classes resented the heavy taxation which was rendered necessary by the war. Brilliant successes might have kindled a spirit of patriotic self-sacrifice, but these successes were still to be won. The parliaments made themselves the organs of local dissatisfaction. In Normandy the opposition of Rouen to the financial edicts of 1637 was only overcome ·by a threatened advance of king and cardinal at the head of an army. In Guienne citizens and peasants rose in armed revolt against the tax-collectors. But the monarchy, as usual, profited by class divisions. The duke of la Valette, one of Richelieu's most active opponents, took command of the royal troops and put down the rebels. To suppress local independence Richelieu extended the use of intendants in 1637, and thus forged the most powerful link in the chain which bound France in servitude to an absolute monarchy.

While the cardinal was engaged in defeating open opposition, his power was threatened by an extraordinary court intrigue, in which religion and love were curiously intermingled. Louis XIII., though constitutionally chaste, had all a Bourbon's delight in feminine society. Alienated from his wife by political and personal antipathy, he was accustomed to cherish a platonic attachment for one of the ladies of his court. For some years his virtuous affection had been fixed upon Mademoiselle de Hautefort, the recognised beauty of Parisian society. But the titular mistress was a devoted admirer of the neglected Anne of Austria, and used all her influence to inspire the king with distrust

of the cardinal, whom she regarded as the chief barrier
between the royal husband and wife. Richelieu and
his supporters were delighted when, in 1635, Louis
transferred his affections to Louise de la Fayette, a
beautiful and pensive brunette, whose personal attrac-
tions were equalled by her piety. The new favourite
was a relative of Father Joseph, and the king's devotion
seemed likely to strengthen the cardinal's ascendency.
But Richelieu's energetic and almost ruthless policy
had little fascination for women, and the innocent
Mademoiselle de la Fayette became the tool of a hostile
cabal. Its leader was a Jesuit, Père Caussin, the royal
confessor, who shared the general distrust of his order
towards the cardinal. But the growing affection of
the king excited the scruples of the maid-of-honour,
and she wished to escape danger by entering the
cloister. This pious resolution was applauded and
encouraged by Richelieu and his supporters. On the
other hand, her relatives and the zealous Caussin strove
to persuade her that she could remain at court without
risk to her virtue. Few more curious incidents are
recorded in French history than this struggle to repress
or to aid the monastic inclinations of a young girl.
At last, whether frightened by royal tenderness, or won
over by the advice of the Dominican agents of Richelieu,
Mademoiselle de la Fayette entered the convent of the
Visitation in the rue St. Antoine (May 19, 1637).
But the battle was only half won. The king, who
applauded while he deplored the resolution of his
mistress, continued to visit her at her convent, and her
denunciations of the cardinal were the more vigorous
now that her virtue was protected by her vows and

the convent bars through which the conversation was conducted. The influence of Père Caussin over the king seemed to be stronger than ever, and an open contest began between the confessor and the minister. But the ties which bound Louis XIII. to the cardinal were too strong to be broken even by the combined weight of priestly and feminine influence. In December 1637 Père Caussin was exiled to Rennes, and the king ceased his visits to the convent of the Visitation.

Meanwhile the war continued to be waged in 1637, as before, with varying success. The death of Ferdinand II. in February made little difference to a struggle of which he had been a principal author. Although the new emperor, Ferdinand III., was more pacifically disposed than his father, he was forced to continue hostilities by the refusal of France and Sweden to recognise an election in which the archbishop of Trier, still a prisoner, had taken no part. Richelieu made his great effort in this year in the Netherlands, whither he sent his friend, the cardinal de la Valette, to co-operate with Frederick Henry. But the militant cardinal did little to justify the confidence of his patron. His only achievements were the capture of two places in Flanders, and the recovery of the frontier fortress of La Chapelle, while the Prince of Orange, more careful of Dutch than of French interests, contented himself with laying siege to Breda, which surrendered in October. These slight successes were more than counterbalanced by losses in Germany and in Italy. In Germany the Imperialists carried all before them. The Swedes were driven from Pomerania, John of Werth took Ehrenbreitstein and Hanau, while Bernhard of Saxe-Weimar, who had over-

run Franche Comté, failed in his attempt to relieve the
last fortress, so that the French lost their last hold on
the coveted province of Elsass.   In Italy the successive
deaths of the dukes of Savoy and Mantua broke up
the coalition which Richelieu had formed against the
Hapsburgs, and the duke of Parma was forced by the
invasion of his duchy to desert the French alliance.
Still more serious was the expulsion of Rohan from the
Grisons, and the recovery of the Valtelline by Spain.
For once, sacrificing religious to political considerations,
the Spaniards offered the Protestants greater concessions than even France had been willing to give.   The
Grisons accepted the bribe, and undertook to rise against
the French, whom they had welcomed as deliverers.
Rohan found his position untenable without native
support, and was forced to evacuate the territory of the
Leagues.   The Hapsburgs thus recovered the interrupted
communication between Tyrol and Lombardy.   The only
counterpoise to these disasters was an event which
must have been peculiarly gratifying to Richelieu.   For
ten years he had laboured to create a French navy, and
in 1636 he had been rewarded by the appearance in the
Mediterranean of a fleet of more than forty vessels.
Nothing was achieved in that year, owing to want of
agreement between the joint commanders, count
Harcourt and the archbishop of Bordeaux.   But in
1637 the fleet sailed from the harbours of Provence, and
after threatening a descent upon Sardinia, returned to
recover the two islands of Lérins, which had been
occupied for two years by the Spaniards.   It was a
small triumph in itself, but it was a relief to the
national pride, and it presaged a great change in the

balance of maritime power in Southern Europe. A powerful French navy could inflict more damage upon the scattered empire of Spain than a succession of the most brilliant victories by land.

The Thirty Years' War had developed, mainly under Richelieu's guidance, into a duel between the houses of Hapsburg and Bourbon, and it was evident that the struggle would be long and desperate. But Richelieu showed no signs of flinching from the task which he had undertaken. He was resolute not to make peace until he had obtained substantial advantages for his country, and until he had broken the power of her rival. France, in spite of financial mismanagement, was the least exhausted of the combatants. The campaign of 1637, although it had not been dazzlingly successful, had at any rate opened the prospect of better things. It was with some confidence that the cardinal set to work to renew his alliance with the Swedes and Bernhard of Saxe-Weimar, while he made strenuous preparations for simultaneous hostilities in Elsass, the Netherlands, Italy, the Spanish frontier, and on the sea. Of so many enterprises, it was impossible that all should be equally successful, but it may be safely affirmed that none was without important and lasting results.

With the year 1638 begins the series of triumphs which have given to Richelieu his almost unequalled reputation as a statesman. If he had died at the end of 1637 he would be remembered as a great home minister, who had crushed the princes, rendered the Huguenots powerless, and supplied the despotic monarchy with an efficient administrative machinery. It

was during the next five years that he earned un-
dying fame as the man who crushed the power of
the house of Hapsburg, secured the ascendency of the
house of Bourbon, and gave an impulse to the history
of Europe which was felt for more than a century after
his death.   And he has the further claim to admiration
that for all his achievements both at home and abroad
he had consciously and intentionally laboured.   Hitherto
we have been tracing the period of preparation and of
partial failure.   Space allows only a brief effort to
point out the direction and extent of his triumphs.

The first, and perhaps in French eyes the greatest of
Richelieu's successes was the conquest of Elsass.   The
hero of this achievement was Bernhard of Saxe Weimar,
a descendant of the Albertine line of Saxony, which
had championed the Protestant cause against Charles V.,
and had paid for its religious zeal by the confiscation of
its territories.   Bernhard's great ambition was to revive
the glories of his family by the acquisition of a German
principality.   It was with this object that he had joined
the Swedes, and after the death of Gustavus Adolphus
he had almost succeeded in erecting a principality in
Franconia.   But the battle of Nordlingen had destroyed
his hopes, and had forced him to accept the French alliance
as the only means of making head against the emperor.
Richelieu had hastened to secure so valuable an ally
by promising him French aid in acquiring the land-
graviate of Elsass, the oldest possession of the Austrian
Hapsburgs.   For three years, owing mainly to the
absorption of France in the Netherlands, Bernhard had
made little advance towards the goal of his endeavours.
But in 1638 Richelieu decided to make Elsass the

principal scene of warfare. He paid up the arrears of the promised subsidies, and promised to make no treaty which did not secure the interests of Bernhard and his army. Thus encouraged, Bernhard hastened to take the field before the winter was over. He had already captured three towns in the Breisgau, and was besieging Rheinfelden when the Imperialists attacked his camp, and after an obstinate struggle forced him to retreat. Nothing daunted by this check, he reorganised his forces, and three days later fell upon the enemy while they were still celebrating their victory. The surprise was completely successful. The Imperialist generals, among whom was the famous John of Werth, fell, with the standards and artillery, into Bernhard's hands. Rheinfelden at once surrendered, and in a few weeks the whole of the Breisgau was reduced to submission.

Bernhard now crossed to the right bank of the Rhine and laid siege to Breisach, the famous fortress which commanded Elsass, and enabled its possessor to control the line of communication between Italy and the Netherlands. The importance of Breisach was fully realised by the Spaniards, and numberless efforts were made to relieve the garrison. But Bernhard succeeded in repulsing all attacks, and on December 19 Breisach was forced to open its gates. The conquest of Elsass was assured. But the advantage to France was by no means so immediate or obvious. Bernhard was fighting his own battle and that of Protestantism, and had no intention of being used as a catspaw by his ally. To the demand that he should recognise French suzerainty over Elsass, he replied that he would not be the first to partition the German Empire. But the erection of an

independent and powerful principality on the French
frontier was by no means in accordance with Richelieu's
wishes. Bernhard seemed likely to prove as inconvenient
and unmanageable as Gustavus Adolphus. But here
fortune came to the assistance of France, as it had done in
1632. Bernhard was eager to secure his new principality
by forcing the emperor to make peace. To effect this
he determined in 1639 to march westward in order to
support the Swedish general, Baner, who was invading
Bohemia. But his health was already broken by
anxieties and fatigue, and he had hardly crossed the
Rhine when he died, on July 15, at the age of thirty-six.
By his will he left his army to the joint command of
his generals, and his territories to whichever of his
brothers would accept them. Bernhard's death was
Richelieu's opportunity. French gold purchased the
allegiance of the German officers and troops, who accepted
a French commander and admitted a French garrison into
Breisach. France had secured a hold upon Elsass which
nothing but a series of signal and unexpected reverses
could compel her to relax. At the same time a fatal
blow was dealt at the cohesion of the Spanish Empire.

In Italy the French triumphs, though rather later,
were hardly less decisive, and they were the more
gratifying because they were directly due to the courage
and generalship of Frenchmen. The death of Victor
Amadeus of Savoy had left the regency for his infant son
in the hands of his widow, Christine. She was a sister
of Louis XIII., but she was anxious to adopt a neutral
attitude in order to secure the interests of her children.
She was, however, forced into a French alliance by
the diplomacy of Richelieu, and by the open hostility of

the Spaniards, who found allies in her brothers-in-law, Thomas and Maurice. Armed with an imperial edict annulling the will of the late duke, and supported by Lleganes, the Spanish governor of Milan, the two princes headed a revolt in Piedmont against Christine. Richelieu did not hesitate to take advantage of the duchess's difficulties to secure the interests of France, and demanded the admission of French garrisons into the capital and chief fortresses of Piedmont. But Christine, whose public conduct was more creditable than her private life, refused to sacrifice the independence of her son's territories even to her own brother. She would only consent to the temporary occupation of three minor fortresses. For the moment she suffered for her patriotism : in the autumn of 1639 both Turin and Nice fell into the hands of her opponents, and she was formally deposed from the regency.

Christine now fled from Piedmont to Savoy, whither she had already sent the young duke for safety. At Grenoble she had a personal interview with Louis XIII. and the cardinal, and again discovered that disinterested assistance was the last thing she could expect from the country of her birth. Richelieu demanded that the young duke should be sent to Paris to be educated, and that the whole of Savoy, together with the places in Piedmont which still held out, should be handed over to French occupation. But the duchess, hard pressed as she was, refused to entrust her son to foreign custody, and insisted upon reserving the fortress of Montmelian as his residence. Richelieu did not conceal his irritation at what he called Christine's obstinacy, but he could not allow the Spaniards to retain their hold on Piedmont.

The cardinal de la Valette, who had been sent to
command in Italy, had died there in September 1639.
He was the only son of Epernon, who was loyal to
Richelieu, and he owed his military employments more
to the minister's gratitude than to his own capacity.
His place was taken by Count Harcourt, the first of the
distinguished French generals who obtained their training in this war.   In 1640 Harcourt commenced the
campaign which laid the foundation for the military
prestige of France.   By a bold march he forced Lleganes,
though at the head of a vastly superior force, to raise
the siege of Casale.   Thence the French returned to
undertake the siege of Turin.   Meanwhile Lleganes
collected all the Spanish troops and advanced to the aid
of Prince Thomas, who commanded the defending garrison.   Harcourt found himself at once besieger and
besieged, and his army was threatened with disease and
starvation.   Fortunately the enemy, instead of harassing
the French and avoiding a direct conflict, tried to crush
them by a combined attack.   After a desperate struggle
under the walls of Turin, Harcourt succeeded not only
in forcing the garrison back to the city, but also in
driving the Spaniards from their position.   After two
months of blockade the garrison could hold out no longer.
A last effort on the part of Lleganes to break through
the besiegers was repulsed, and on September 22
Turin opened its gates.   " I would rather be Count
Harcourt than emperor ! " said the captive John of
Werth, when he heard the news of this achievement.
In November Christine returned to her capital amidst the
applause of the citizens.   By the end of another year the
Spaniards had been completely driven from Piedmont.

For the victories in Italy Richelieu was indebted to the capacity of subordinates, whom he had selected and inspired, but whose actions he could not direct. For the naval triumphs of France he may claim far more personal glory, as he was the virtual creator of the French navy. Hitherto the only achievement of the fleet had been the capture of the Lérins, and there had been no attempt to meet the Spaniards in open battle. But the year 1638 witnessed the first serious blow to that maritime ascendency without which Spain could hardly defend its own territories, much less prove formidable to foreign states. On August 22 Archbishop Sourdis attacked and almost destroyed a Spanish squadron off Guetaria in the Bay of Biscay. Only a week later fifteen French vessels under Pont-Courlay, a nephew of Richelieu, assaulted an equal number of Spanish ships near Genoa. The struggle was long and exhausting, but the superior artillery of the French gave them an advantage at close quarters, and their victory was crowned by the capture of the Spanish admiral. This success, though smaller, was even more significant than that of Guetaria, because the Spanish power had, since Lepanto, no rival on the Mediterranean, whereas in the northern seas it was already threatened by the growing navy of the United Provinces. In 1639 events at sea were still more decisive. A large Spanish fleet succeeded in evading the watchfulness of Sourdis, and reached the English Channel. There it met the Dutch under Martin Tromp, and after fighting for two days the Spaniards sought the Downs and the shelter of the English coast. While Charles I. was higgling with Spain about the price to be paid for

his protection, Richelieu succeeded in conveying to
Tromp an intimation to disregard the threats of
England. Nothing loth, the Dutch admiral sailed
against the Spanish fleet, and almost completely destroyed it (October 11). Barely ten of the great
galleons succeeded in reaching Dunkirk in safety.
Spain had experienced no such crushing disaster since
the loss of the great Armada. With its fleet shattered
and Breisach in the hands of the French, it was almost
impossible to send assistance to the Netherlands.

Since the treaty of 1629 Richelieu had little to fear
from the hostility of England. Charles I. seemed
determined to maintain an inexpensive if inglorious
neutrality, and he was alienated from Spain by the
steady refusal to do anything for the Palatine family.
But the growing naval power of France excited misgivings in England. Charles was indignant at the
insult to the English flag in the Downs, and Henrietta
Maria was not disinclined to espouse the cause of her
mother against the minister who condemned her to
life-long exile. But Richelieu had weapons ready to
hand against the English king, and he did not scruple
to use them. French agents and French money had
no small part in stirring up that Scotch rebellion which
dealt the first fatal blow to Stuart despotism. And
when the expenses and failures of the war forced Charles
at last to summon the Long Parliament, Richelieu did
not hesitate to establish relations with the opposition
party, which had less cause than the king to favour
Spain. No doubt the Great Rebellion would have
arisen if Richelieu had never lived, but he had some
share in moulding the actual events which led to it. It

was even reported and believed that when Charles endeavoured to seize the five members, the warning which enabled them to escape came from the French ambassador. The minister who did more than any other man to establish absolutism in France may claim to have assisted—from purely selfish motives—in the vindication of liberty in England.

The same keen insight which enabled Richelieu to appreciate and make use of the elements of discontent and opposition in England and Scotland was equally apparent in his relations with the Spanish peninsula. Spain, unlike France, was never a united state. The Hapsburgs were primarily kings of Castile, and they ruled the other parts of the peninsula as dependent provinces, no better off than Naples or Milan. This policy was not likely to conciliate a population in which local prejudices and traditions were always stronger than central interests. The two extremes of the peninsula, Portugal and Catalonia, were especially alienated by a government which trampled upon their pride and their aspirations to independence. Olivares, the all-powerful minister of Philip IV., saw the weakness of Spain, but could not devise the proper remedy. He attributed the superiority of France, quite rightly, to its greater unity and centralisation, and thought to exalt his own country by imitating the government of his rival. But it was not easy to make the bonds more tolerable merely by tightening them. The only result of his premature experiment was to provoke a double rebellion, which France was quite ready to ferment and to use for its own advantage.

The local militia of Catalonia had loyally defended

the little province of Roussillon against French invasion in 1639. But the people resented the outrages of the Castilian troops, who were quartered upon them during the winter. Early in 1640 Olivares issued an edict ordering the enrolment of all men capable of bearing arms to serve wherever they should be sent. This was contrary to the traditional privileges of the provinces, and excited a general revolt. As the government of Madrid would make no concessions, the rebels turned for assistance to France. Richelieu had no scruples about the legitimacy of a revolt which served his plans, and promised to send officers and 8000 men to aid the Catalans. Nor was a mere diversion of the enemy's attention the only result at which he aimed. In January 1641 a treaty was arranged by which the Catalans were to become not only the allies but the subjects of France, on condition that their liberties should be respected. The Pyrenees had never been a boundary, and for centuries Spanish rule had extended north of the mountain range. Now France threatened to advance to the Ebro, once the limit of the power of Charles the Great.

The example of Catalonia was promptly followed by Portugal, which had been annexed by Philip II. in 1580, but had never acquiesced in the rule of its conquerors. From the first declaration of war Richelieu had reckoned upon Portuguese assistance, and his agents had been busy in encouraging and stirring up discontent. Probably the revolt would have begun sooner but for the moderation or timidity of the duke of Braganza, the largest landholder in Portugal and the representative of the old royal line. But in 1640 circumstances were too favourable to be neglected. The nobles refused to obey the order of Olivares to march against Catalonia, and could only avoid the penalty of disobedience by rebellion. The scruples of the duke of Braganza were overcome by French representations, and in December he was proclaimed king as John IV. Never was a revolution accomplished with greater ease or unanimity. The first act of the new king was to conclude a treaty with France, which promised to aid him against Spain, while he pledged himself to conclude no treaty without French approval.

In the Netherlands events were not so rapid or decisive as elsewhere; but here also the year 1640 witnessed an important triumph for France. In June the French army laid siege to Arras, the strongly-fortified capital of the border province of Artois. Artois was an ancient fief of France, but had been freed from vassalage by Charles V. The Cardinal Infant and the duke of Lorraine tried to harass the besiegers by occupying the adjacent country and cutting off supplies. Richelieu himself went to Amiens to superintend the sending of reinforcements and provisions to Arras. A regular army was formed to conduct the convoy. Before it could arrive the Spaniards made a desperate attack upon the French camp, but were repulsed. This failure was decisive. On August 9 the town of Arras was surrendered, and the province of Artois was declared to be reunited to the French crown. It was a conquest which France was not likely to relinquish.

The aspect of affairs had undergone a startling change since 1636. In that year the Spaniards had

been victors on French soil, and their advance had
excited a panic in the French capital. In 1640 France
was not only secure against invasion, but its frontier
had been advanced in the east, in the north, and in the
south, and its great rival, Spain, was threatened with
imminent dissolution. The connection with the Netherlands was already destroyed, and the French fleet in the
Mediterranean made communication with Italy difficult
and dangerous. In the peninsula itself two provinces
were in open revolt, and one of them seemed likely to
become a part of France. The man who, in five years,
had produced such marvellous results was Richelieu.

While the cardinal's foreign policy had been attended with such gratifying success, an event had
occurred at home which he regarded with even greater
satisfaction. The essential weakness of Richelieu's
position was the fact that Louis XIII. was childless,
and that the heir to the throne was his inveterate
opponent, the feeble and vicious Gaston of Orleans.
But on September 5, 1638, after twenty-three years of
married life, Anne of Austria rendered her first service
to the minister whom she detested by giving birth to a
dauphin, afterwards Louis XIV. Richelieu presented
a diamond rose to the messenger who brought him the
welcome news, and all France shared in his exultation.
In 1640 the succession was still further secured by the
birth of a second son, the ancestor of the house of
Orleans.

One misfortune clouded the felicity of the grand
period of Richelieu's career. In December 1638, just
after the news of the capture of Breisach, he lost Father
Joseph, "his prop and consolation," as he called him in

the first fervour of his grief. Richelieu's detractors
have not hesitated to make the most of the obscurity
which covers the relations between these two men.
They have contended that Father Joseph was the brain
and Richelieu the arm ; that the red cardinal was only
the marionette who danced before the public, while the
grey cardinal pulled the strings. To such assertions
or innuendoes no answer is possible except that there
is no evidence for it, and against it we have not only
antecedent improbability, but the fact that Richelieu's
policy and character show no signs of vacillation or
weakness after the death of his friend. The only
reasonable conclusion is that the Capuchin monk was
the most able and perhaps the most trusted of the few
confidential agents whom Richelieu collected round
him, but that there is no ground for believing that he
was more than a familiar adviser whose counsel was
always valued, but not always adopted.

CHAPTER VIII

DOMESTIC GOVERNMENT

THE foremost statesmen of history may be roughly
divided into two chief classes.   Some are great diplom-
atists, endowed with a natural gift for understanding
and influencing the relations between the great states
of their time, and they employ this gift to such purpose
as to secure the prestige and the material advancement
of their own country, and thereby profoundly influence
the general history of the world.   Others concentrate
their attention mainly upon domestic problems : either
upon economic questions, such as the development of
trade, or manufactures, or colonisation ; or upon more

purely political questions, such as the relations of classes
to each other or to the crown, the extension or limita-
tion of local independence, the widening or narrowing
of the basis of government. It is one of Richelieu's
claims to exceptional distinction that he belongs to both
these classes. For good or for evil, he left an inefface-
able mark both upon the general history of Europe and
upon the internal development of France. It may be
contended that he was more successful as a diplomatist
than as a ruler of France, that he was too much absorbed
in foreign politics to give sufficient attention to the
solution of domestic problems; but there can be no
doubt that his influence was equally great in both
departments of government.

The aims of Richelieu's domestic policy are extremely
simple, and they have been described by himself with
equal point and clearness in the " brief narration of the
great actions of the king," which he drew up towards
the close of his ministry. " When your Majesty resolved
to admit me to his council and to a share in his confidence, I can say with truth that the Huguenots divided
the State with the monarchy, that the nobles behaved
as if they were not subjects, and that the chief governors
of provinces acted as if they had been independent
sovereigns. . . . I then undertook to employ all my
energy and all the authority that you were pleased to
give me to ruin the Huguenot faction, to humble the
pride of the nobles, to reduce all your subjects to their
duty, and to exalt your name to its proper position
among foreign nations." Hostile critics have contended
that the dangers from the Huguenots and the nobles
were less than Richelieu would have us believe, but no

one has denied that he made it his first object to establish the unity of France, that he conceived a strong monarchy to be the only basis of that unity, and that he set himself resolutely to remove or destroy all obstacles to the direct and efficient exercise of the central power.

Richelieu's treatment of the Huguenots has been already sufficiently described. He deprived them of their exceptional privileges and securities, reduced them to political impotence, but left them in the enjoyment of religious liberty. The result was that many of the nobles, who had espoused the reformed doctrines mainly as a means of recovering independence, returned to orthodoxy in the hope of gaining court favour. An orderly and governing mind could hardly fail to appreciate the value of uniformity of belief and worship as a bulwark of national unity, and there were not wanting advisers to urge upon Richelieu that a little politic pressure might result in the extinction of a sect with which he had scant reason to sympathise. But the cardinal steadily refused to risk the undoing of the work he had accomplished and to revive religious discord by persecution. His complaint against the Huguenots had been that they were Protestants first and Frenchmen afterwards; if they would only consent to be Frenchmen in the first place, and to regard patriotic devotion as their primary duty, he had no desire to alienate them once more from the state by attempting to enforce religious conformity. His moderation was rewarded with complete success. The Huguenots showed their gratitude by becoming in the next generation not only the most industrious and thrifty, but also the most loyal subjects of the crown.

The list of great commanders whose ability turned the
scale in the struggle between France and Spain would
be sadly diminished, both in numbers and in brilliance,
if it had not included such famous Huguenots as
Gassion, de la Force, de Rohan, Duquesne, and Turenne.

The Vicomte d'Avenel, in his great work on
Richelieu et la Monarchie Absolue, has endeavoured to
defend the French nobles from the charges of factious
disloyalty which constitute the sole justification of
Richelieu's harsh treatment of their order.   But his
special pleading, learned and ingenious as it is, breaks
down before the bare facts of history during the religious
wars, the regency of Mary de Medici, and the Fronde.
It is impossible for any unprejudiced reader of those
periods to avoid the conclusion that as a class the
nobles were the most dangerous and useless part of the
population.   Their pretensions to lawless independence
were equally inconsistent with the efficiency of the
central government and with the prosperity of the
people.   They had ceased to perform most of the
duties which had devolved upon them in the days of the
feudal system, yet they retained all the privileges and
exemptions which they had gained in consideration of
their discharge of these duties.   The relations of the
chief nobles with Gaston of Orleans and the queen-
mother, together with the fact that the foreign enemies
of France openly encouraged and exulted in these
divisions, would have justified Richelieu's attitude on
the simple ground of self-defence, even if it were impossible to find any higher motive for his actions.

The power of the French nobles rested mainly upon
a triple basis : (1) their strongly-fortified castles, each

of which required a separate siege for its reduction;
(2) their contempt for ordinary jurisdiction, and their
claim to settle their own disputes by what had once
been their recognised right—private war; (3) the power
which they exercised in the provinces through their
position as governors.   With that insight which is
always the highest proof of statesmanship, Richelieu
struck directly at the foundations, confident that if they
could be overthrown the superstructure would topple
down of its own accord.   In 1626 two important edicts
were issued.   One ordered the destruction of all
fortresses, except such as were needed for the defence of
the frontiers, and forbade in the future the fortification
of private houses.   The other prohibited duelling on
pain of death.   The first of these edicts was carried out
amidst the applause of burghers and peasants.   It has
been urged that the compulsory demolition was unnecessary, and therefore of slight importance, that the
changed habits of the nobles required comfort rather
than fortifications, and that the later style of baronial
residence would have come in of its own accord without
any action on the part of the government.   But this
argument carries with it its own refutation.   The
changed habits of the nobles were the result, not the
cause, of their political impotence; and that impotence
arose from the disappearance of the old sense of
impunity, to which the loss of defensible walls un-
questionably contributed.   The edict against duels, in
spite of the severity dealt out to Bouteville and des
Chapelles, was not enforced with anything like the
same stringency.   Richelieu himself had too much of the
sentiment of his noble birth and his military training

not to feel a real sympathy for the traditional method of defending personal honour. No execution for which he was responsible cost him more hesitation and misgivings than that of Bouteville, and he devotes several pages of his *Memoirs* to a regretful estimate of his merits and misfortunes. It was rather the general character of Richelieu's administration than the letter of any particular edict which caused the gradual decline of the practice of duelling.

When Richelieu entered the ministry in 1624 he found the chief provinces divided among nineteen governors, all of them belonging to the highest rank of nobility. These regarded their posts as private and heritable property to be administered for their personal interests. Whenever they had occasion to quarrel with the court, it was to their province that they retreated, either as a secure asylum or as a source of strength for attack. By the time of the cardinal's death, only four of these nineteen governors retained their position. The rest had been removed to make room for officials whom the minister could trust. And a terrible lesson of the duty and necessity of obedience had been taught to these local rulers by the defeat and execution of Montmorency in his own province of Languedoc. But by far the greatest blow to the authority of the nobles was dealt by the appointment of intendants. A small literature has arisen in recent years on the subject of the origin of these famous officials. An edict of 1635 which had long been regarded as marking the definite creation of intendants has been conclusively proved to have no reference to them. It has been further proved that *maîtres des requêtes* of the royal council had been fre-

quently sent out to the provinces in the sixteenth century
with the title of intendant, and with special instructions
to supervise and control local administration.   But the
tradition which regards Richelieu as their real author
has still a substantial foundation.   It was he who made
the intendants permanent officials, who extended them
to the whole kingdom, and gave them their complete
functions as intendants of justice, police, and finance.
No single edict determined their appointment or defined
their powers, but gradually they obtained the supreme
control of all departments of administration, and became
the recognised channel of communication between their
districts and the royal council.   The jealousy which
they inspired among the privileged classes is illustrated
by the fact that one of the first demands of the Fronde
was for their suppression.   But under Louis XIV. they
were restored, to become the agents of that efficient,
if excessive centralisation, which constituted at once
the strength and the weakness of the later Bourbon
monarchy.   The nobles retained their dignity and
their revenues as provincial governors, but all substantial authority passed to the middle-class officials, who
had neither the means nor the temptation to resist the
crown.

It would take too long to examine in detail all the
measures taken by Richelieu to simplify and centralise
the government of France.   He suppressed the ancient
and dignified offices of constable and admiral because
they gave their holders a power too great to be safely
entrusted to a subject.   He never summoned the States-
General, and he sternly checked the political pretensions
of that most interesting and unique of judicial courts,

the Parliament of Paris. By an edict of 1641 the parliament was forbidden to take any cognisances of affairs of state, unless its advice was specially asked by the king; all edicts on matters of government or administration are to be registered at once without opposition or debate; on financial matters the parliament is forbidden to introduce amendments; any remonstrances it may wish to make must be presented at once, and if they are rejected, registration is to follow as a matter of course; finally, the old formula of refusal, "we ought not and cannot," is expressly prohibited as injurious to the authority of the prince. Nor was Richelieu content with this suppression of political powers, to which the claim was of more than doubtful validity; he also encroached upon the undoubted rights of jurisdiction which the court had always possessed. In spite of the vigorous and well-justified protests, both of the parliament and of the accused, the trial of prominent political offenders was in all cases withdrawn from the cognisance of the supreme law court, and entrusted to extraordinary commissions nominated for each case. This exceptional jurisdiction, which enabled Richelieu to give a dangerous latitude and vagueness to offences against the state, was one of the most arbitrary and least defensible features of his administration.

Of the local liberties which had survived in some parts of France Richelieu showed himself the bitter enemy. Most of the provinces were *pays d'élection*, *i.e.* they were divided into districts in which the assessment and collection of taxes were vested in royal officials called *élus*. But several provinces had retained representative institutions, either by custom or by special agreement made at the time of their annexation to the crown. The chief of these *pays d'états* were Languedoc, Normandy, Brittany, Burgundy, Provence, and Dauphiné. The composition and powers of the provincial estates varied in innumerable details, but all had one common privilege : they made their own financial bargains with the crown, and they appointed their own officials to assess and collect their contributions to the state. The suppression in 1629 of the Huguenot revolt in Languedoc gave Richelieu an opportunity for attempting the suppression of this privilege, and edicts were issued to extend the division into *élections* to all the provinces of France. These edicts were finally enforced in Normandy and Dauphiné. In the latter the estates were altogether abolished, and in Normandy, though the estates continued to meet till their final suppression in 1666, they lost all practical power. In the other provinces the edicts provoked strenuous remonstrances and resistance, to which Richelieu, warned by Montmorency's rising in Languedoc, found it advisable to yield. In Languedoc, Burgundy, and Provence the *élections* were abolished, but these provinces had to purchase the concession by heavy money payments and by accepting conditions which deprived the provincial estates of much of their independence. For instance, in Languedoc, by far the most important of the *pays d'états*, the estates were only allowed to meet every other year ; their session was limited to fifteen days, and they were strictly forbidden to levy any tax or loan without the royal approval. In Brittany alone, where the composition of the estates was least democratic, and where Richelieu had special authority, both as governor and

as head of the maritime administration, no special
attempt was made to harass the provincial assembly,
which indeed had shown a desire to aid rather than to
impede the minister's policy. But even in Brittany
some changes were made to the advantage of the crown.
The nobles lost the right of personal attendance, and
could only appear when authorised by royal letters-
patent, and the towns which were to send deputies to
the meeting were to be selected on each occasion by the
governor. In this connection, too, it must be remembered that the institution of intendants contributed to
strengthen the control of the central government over
both *pays d'états* and *pays d'élections*.

One obvious result of Richelieu's policy was to throw
a vast increase of work upon the royal council, and
it was necessary to improve its organisation so as to
enable it to meet its enlarged duties and responsibilities. Richelieu's arrangements, which lasted, with slight
changes in detail, till the fall of the monarchy, may be
instructively compared with the organisation of the
Privy Council undertaken by the Tudor kings under
the pressure of similar necessities. To render the
conduct of business regular and uniform the council
was split into sections, which met on special days for the
consideration of particular departments. On Tuesdays
was held the *conseil des dépêches*, which was responsible
for the provincial administration. To it were sent all
reports from the governors and other local officers,
and its functions resemble those of our Home Office.
The *conseil des finances* sat twice a week—on Wednes-
days, to consider all questions connected with assessment and expenditure, and on Thursdays, to hear all

appeals on financial matters, either from officials or from private individuals.   On Saturdays was held the *conseil des parties* or the *conseil privé*.   This was a purely judicial body.   Before it were brought appeals from other courts to the crown, and a number of cases of first instance, especially those in which officials were interested, which were evoked from the ordinary courts to the royal council.   These councils must not be regarded as distinct bodies, but as parts of the same body.   The great officers of state, the chancellor, the *surintendant des finances*, and the four secretaries of state, were members of all the divisions, and so were many of the ordinary councillors.   The business of each section was prepared and reported upon by a number of *maîtres des requêtes*, who took it in turns to serve at the council for three months at a time.   At other times they were employed in special commissions in the royal service. These men formed the nursery of French administrators, and it was from among them that the intendants were always selected.

But this elaborate organisation was only concerned with the routine work of administration.   The *conseil du roy*, like the English Privy Council under the later Stuarts, had become too numerous and clumsy a body to provide that secrecy and concentration which a despotism always requires, and especially for foreign affairs.   The same motives which led in England to the growth of the Cabinet, produced a similar institution in France, which is variously known as the *conseil d'état*, the *conseil d'en haut*, *conseil étroit* or *conseil privé*.

It is impossible to describe Richelieu as the founder of this institution, which grew out of obvious necessities ;

but it was he who gave it the form and the importance which it retained till the Revolution. The council of state—to choose one out of its numerous appellations— had the sole consideration of foreign affairs, which had formerly gone to the *conseil des dépêches*, and it possessed the real initiative and decisive voice in all domestic matters. Its members, who were always nominated by the king, were called *ministres d'état*. The chief officers of state were usually, but not necessarily, included in the council, but the king often admitted men who held no special office. The king himself presided, and in his absence the first minister. The powers of the council were in appearance very great. It quashed the decisions of ordinary courts, it evoked cases for its own consideration, and appointed extraordinary judicial commissions. It issued the edicts which became law on registration by the parliament. It could make peace or war, determine the amount and method of taxation, and supervise the conduct of all other administrative bodies. But these enormous powers were in reality not the powers of the council but of the crown. The ministers of state had no other function than to advise. There was no voting, and no decision by a majority. The members stated their opinion, often in the form of a written memoir, but the king decided at his own pleasure.

Thus Richelieu had erected an administrative system which survived the attacks of nobles and parliament in the Fronde, and justified the boast attributed to Louis XIV., *l'État c'est moi!* It is usual, though of doubtful fairness, to hold the cardinal responsible for the fact that succeeding kings abused the powers bequeathed to them, or at any rate failed to use them for the best advantage of their country. It is the inherent vice of despotism that no human ingenuity can provide a succession of men wise and virtuous enough to be intrusted with that omnipotence which in the hands of a perfect ruler may be for a moment the best form of government in the world. Englishmen have, except for a short interval, preferred a government in which there is more balance of forces, more complicated machinery, and less individual initiative and responsibility. Such a system has many unquestionable defects; it is less simple, less logical, and less easy to work than a centralised despotism; but it has the supreme merit of being safer, of leaving less to chance, of resting upon the average capacity of the many, rather than upon the possibility of exceptional capacity in one. Those critics who condemn Richelieu for the ultimate failure of French despotism are of opinion that he ought to have founded, or tried to found, a constitutional government in France like that which gradually grew up in England. Instead of doing "everything for the people, and nothing by the people," he should have allowed the subjects some voice in their own government. To this criticism there is one simple and overwhelming answer : it was quite impossible. ·It would require a long analysis of French history and French institutions to furnish conclusive proof of this assertion, but it can be so established beyond question. Ever since the thirteenth century there had been an incurable twist against constitutionalism. The secret of the successful beginning of parliamentary government in England is to be found in the

alliance of classes against the crown, which begins with
the great struggle to extort the charter from John.
Such an alliance is conspicuously absent in France,
where from the thirteenth to the eighteenth century
there is no single instance of a league between the
nobles and the third estate to secure an interest common
to both. The jealous hostility of classes in France
enabled the crown to play off one against the other,
and thus to raise itself to unchallenged supremacy.
Geographical needs and the long struggles, first with
England and afterwards with Spain, all contributed to
the triumph of the monarchy. No statesman, however great, can free himself from the influence of
historical development, nor can he work with other
instruments than those which are supplied to him from
the past. In France there were two institutions which
at one time or another claimed what we should call
constitutional powers. The States-General, after a
brief triumph in the middle of the fourteenth century,
proved a complete and hopeless failure. The division
into three orders, each more zealous for its selfish
interests than for the general welfare, and the inability
of the third estate to make its influence felt against
the ascendency of nobles and clergy, condemned this
assembly to sterile impotence. Richelieu himself, as
has been seen, was a prominent member of the States-
General of 1614, and had seen enough to convince him
that the success of France was not to be sought there.
No similar assembly met till the eve of the Revolution.
The disappearance of the States-General gave increased
prominence and importance to the Parliament of Paris,
which endeavoured to fill the gap thus created. This

hereditary corporation of judges aspired to emulate the English legislature, with which it had nothing in common but the name. The practice of registration enabled them to claim a right first of remonstrance and afterwards of veto on all legislation, and their independence of royal nomination or dismissal gave this claim an importance which it would not otherwise have possessed. But it would be the grossest mistake to argue from the spirited and often just opposition of the Parliament to despotism that its members had any sympathy with popular wishes, or any understanding of popular needs. The Parliament of Paris, as was conclusively shown on the eve of the Revolution, was really the last and firmest stronghold of official prejudices and class privileges. If Richelieu ever seriously considered the alternatives he would have been right in deciding that it was better to trust the future of France to the monarchy than to a narrow and bigoted bureaucracy. In the one there was a chance of salvation, in the other there was none.

The criterion by which Richelieu's government should be tested is to be sought, not in an estimate of the successes or blunders of the later Bourbons, but in an examination as to whether Richelieu himself made the best use of the authority which he established. That his foreign policy was prudent and far-sighted, and that it was guided by a single-minded desire to promote the interests of his country, has been generally admitted both by Frenchmen and by foreigners. But it is not easy to be equally positive about his domestic administration. Many of his measures may doubtless be praised without reserve. He revived the military

organisation, which had fallen into chaos during the
disorders of the religious wars. The steps which he
took to increase the numbers of the army by an improved system of recruiting, to develop and systematise
the commissariat, and to enforce strict discipline, anticipated the more thorough reforms of le Tellier and
Louvois, and began the process which made the French
army for half a century the finest fighting force in the
world. Still more personal credit is due to the naval
administration, to which Richelieu gave strenuous and
unflagging attention. When he came into office there
was practically no navy at all, and in time of war the
government had to depend upon the vessels it could
hire from individuals. When Sully, under Henry IV.,
was sent on an embassy to London, he had to make
the voyage in an English vessel, and we have seen that
Richelieu, in his first measures against the Huguenots,
was forced to employ borrowed ships from England and
Holland. Thus the whole task of naval construction,
of the forming and training of efficient crews, had to
be begun from the very beginning. But Richelieu's
energetic will was equal to all difficulties. By the time
of his death France possessed thirty-two men of war in
the Mediterranean, and twenty-four on the Atlantic
coast, without counting the smaller vessels. And this
force had shown itself fully capable on more than one
occasion of holding its own against the naval power of
Spain, which had hitherto been without a rival in
Southern Europe. At the same time special attention
was paid to the fortification of naval ports. The defences of Toulon in the south, and of Havre in the north,
were immensely strengthened. Richelieu's special in-

terest in Poitou led him to exaggerate the importance
of Brouage, on which large sums of money were wasted;
but he more than redeemed this mistake by creating
the port of Brest, which was destined in the future to
be the great French arsenal on the Atlantic. It is
further to his credit that he. recognised the important
truth that the only sound basis of naval power is to be
found in a mercantile marine, and that he spared no
pains to extend French commerce and colonisation. He
protected Mediterranean traders against the pirates
of Algiers, Tunis, and Morocco, and he opened fresh
markets in the north by commercial treaties with
Russia, Sweden, and Denmark. His colonial policy was
marred by the practice, common to all statesmen of
that day, of entrusting colonial enterprise entirely to
exclusive companies. These corporations, by which
privileged individuals were protected at the expense of
the general body of consumers, were extremely unsuccessful in French hands, partly through their excessive
dependence upon state patronage and control, and partly
through their total neglect of agriculture, and the consequent failure to form permanent and prosperous
French settlements. Still, in spite of the inherent
defects of the methods he employed, Richelieu's ministry
marks a notable era in the history of French colonies.
His support secured the restoration to Canada of
Quebec and Nova Scotia, which had been seized by the
English, and his encouragement also led to the establishment of French settlements on the coast of Guiana
and in the West Indian islands of St. Christopher, Mar-
tinique, Guadaloupe, and St. Domingo, and in the east
to the first attempt to occupy Madagascar.

But against these measures, which were well-intentioned if not always wise, must be set an almost complete neglect of the internal wellbeing of France. In the history of the progress of French agriculture and manufactures. there is a distinct and lamentable gap between the time of Sully and that of Colbert. In spite of the strongly-worded protests of the third estate in 1614, Richelieu left production hampered by the system of guilds and privileged corporations, and he made no attempt to remove or limit the provincial customs duties which acted as a barrier to internal trade, and as a hindrance to the complete realisation of national interests and unity. But by far the most serious charge against Richelieu's domestic government is based on his complete failure to reform the abuses of the financial administration of France. The direct taxes, from which the privileged classes were wholly exempt, were extremely oppressive in their incidence, especially in those provinces where the *taille* was levied on personal and not on real property. The indirect taxes, assessed for the most part on the selling prices of commodities, were likewise extremely unequal, and constituted a direct discouragement to exchange. The *gabelle* on salt was perhaps the most ludicrously iniquitous tax recorded in the history of any civilised community. The sale of offices, a practice which had been going on for more than a century, had given rise to a disguised national debt, contracted on the most extravagant and ruinous terms. The practice of farming the indirect taxes, and the constant insufficiency of the revenue to meet the expenditure, had placed the government at the mercy of the financiers, who were accustomed to make large fortunes at the expense of the tax-payers. The secrecy and consequent disorder of the public accounts had facilitated fraud and peculation, and the reckless concessions to rebellious nobles during the king's minority had more than undone the reforms which Sully had introduced under Henry IV.

Richelieu was not a trained economist, and many of the evils of the financial system were doubtless less obvious in the seventeenth than they are in the nineteenth century. But that contemporaries were fully alive to some of the worst abuses, and were clamorous for their removal, is fully established by the *cahiers* of the third estate in 1614. That Richelieu himself was equally alive to the necessity of reform is proved, not so much by the dubious evidence of the so-called *Testament Politique*, as by numerous passages in his *Memoirs*, and by the detailed proposals which he submitted to the king in 1625. It is equally certain that Richelieu was the only minister in French history who possessed sufficient authority and strength of will to carry through a sweeping measure of financial reform against the interested opposition of the privileged classes, who in the end succeeded in maintaining the old abuses till they were swept away by the Revolution. A few tentative measures were taken in his earlier years, such as the reduction of the *taille* by 600,000 francs, and the appointment of a chamber of justice which mulcted the financiers of some of their ill-gotten gains. But these Acts led to no permanent improvement, and in the meantime the worst evils, the sale of offices, the *gabelle*, and the system of the *ferme*, were left absolutely untouched. And under the growing pressure of military expenditure all idea of reform was ultimately abandoned. Every method of raising the revenue was strained to the uttermost. The opposition of the parliaments, of the provincial estates, and of armed rebellion, as in the case of the famous *Nus-pieds* in Normandy, was ruthlessly suppressed. New offices were created for the purpose of selling them, and direct loans were raised at an ever-increasing rate of interest. The result was that after Richelieu's death the queen regent found that the revenues of the next three years had been already spent.

It has, of course, been urged by Richelieu's defenders that the greatest and most industrious statesman cannot do everything, and that a period of almost incessant war does not offer a favourable opportunity for the introduction of financial reforms. To the second argument it may be answered that Richelieu was in office for ten years before France was involved in war on a large scale, and that if he had set himself in those ten years to remedy acknowledged abuses, and to abolish or restrict harmful and obsolete privileges, he would have immensely increased the ability of the country to stand the strain of the vastly-increased expenditure after 1635. And to the first argument the possible answer has still more weight. Like many other notable rulers, Richelieu was extremely jealous of the display of any independence or initiative on the part of his colleagues. In choosing them, he did not look for ability or even honesty so much as for absolute submission to himself. The same autocratic assumption that impelled him to control from Paris the operations of generals in the field, led him at home to surround

himself, as time went on, with useful tools rather than
with men of marked capacity. To this must be
attributed the rapid though temporary decline of France
after his death. In no branch of administration, except
in diplomacy, did Richelieu leave behind him a ready-
trained politician capable of filling his place. It is not
too much to say that the Fronde would never have
taken place if Richelieu had thought more of securing
efficiency in those departments to which he could not
give sufficient personal attention, and less of con-
centrating all authority in his own hands.

This concentration may have been partially forced
upon Richelieu by his isolation, and by the necessity of
defending his authority against jealous opponents, but it
had none the less disastrous results to the administration of finance. On the fall of la Vieuville, the duties
of *surintendant* were divided between Michel Marillac
and Champigny, of whom the former was undoubtedly
the ablest of Richelieu's colleagues, and had also a
genuine desire for reform. In 1626 Marillac was appointed keeper of the seals, and the finances were intrusted to the marquis d'Effiat. On his death in 1632
the system of dual control was revived by the appointment of Bullion and Bouthillier, whose chief qualification was that they were the docile agents of the
cardinal, and after the former's death Bouthillier
remained in office alone. These ministerial changes
are coincident with a steady decline in the management
of French finance. The short-lived and rather half-
hearted reforms belong to the period of Marillac's
tenure of office. Under d'Effiat some measure of order
was preserved, and the public credit was maintained,

and in some respects improved, in spite of an increase
of taxation. The reckless multiplication both of exactions and of indebtedness belongs to the time of Bullion
and Bouthillier.

There can be no doubt that Richelieu's neglect of
the paramount duty of financial reform, whether it be
condemned or excused, was of decisive importance for
the future history of France. No subsequent minister
was strong enough to cleanse the Augean stable, and
the partial improvement effected by Colbert was soon
effaced by the lavish expenditure of Louis XIV. on
luxury and war. Throughout the eighteenth century
the efforts of France were crippled by the burden of a
chronic deficit which threatened to bring the state to
bankruptcy. It is impossible to exaggerate the importance to a state of a wholesome and efficient financial
system. France was able to get the better of Spain
because the economic condition of Spain was even worse
than her own. But the decline of Spain and the
exhaustion of Holland left France face to face with
England, and the two states waged a long and desperate
struggle for commercial and colonial expansion. The
financial system of mediæval England, though not so
full of abuses as that of France, was almost equally
inefficient and stationary. The greatest boon which the
Commonwealth conferred upon England was the abolition of the antiquated methods of taxation, and the
substitution of a system which, whatever its faults in
detail, had the supreme merit of making the national
revenue proportionate to the nation's wealth. Among
the many causes which helped England to gain the victory
over France on the sea, in America and in India, not the

least important was the vast superiority of her financial administration, which enabled her to defray with comparative ease an expenditure which reduced her rival to exhaustion and despair. This superiority might never have existed if Richelieu or his colleagues had been far-sighted enough to grapple with problems from which they deliberately turned their attention.

Although Richelieu deliberately set himself to establish absolutism and to free the monarchy from all effective restraints upon its action, it would be a great error to suppose that he recklessly disregarded public opinion, or that he failed to appreciate the strength which any government obtains by conciliating its support. It is true that he would have nothing to do with the States-General, but he summoned two important meetings of Notables, one in 1626 to parade the national sanction of his anti-papal action in the matter of the Valtelline, and the other in 1627 to strengthen his domestic position after the first conspiracy against him had ended in the execution of Chalais. Of course these meetings were carefully packed, and they were allowed no legislative powers. His motives for their convention were much the same as those which induced Simon de Montfort to summon the parliament of 1265, or Philip the Fair to hold the first sessions of the States-General. At the same time the Notables were allowed, especially in 1627, considerable latitude and liberty of discussion, and their debates gave to the measures and schemes of the government a publicity which a less enlightened despotism might have considered both dangerous and degrading.

The same desire to satisfy and gain over opinion is

apparent in his patronage of literature, though here
personal tastes and interests combined to influence his
action. He surrounded himself with a small regiment
of learned scribes, whom he employed to produce
treatises in support of his views on such subjects as the
claims of the crown to foreign territories, or the proper
relations of church and state. The *Memoirs* and the
Succincte Narration, which constitute his own chief contributions to literature, were probably drafted in the
first instance by these subordinates, though he reserved
the task of revision for himself. But his interest was
by no means confined to the serious and practical uses
of literary composition. He was himself an indefatigable
writer of versified dramas, though his industry could
not command success nor his authority applause. His
personal failure, however, did not make him meanly
jealous of more fortunate followers of the Muses.
Nearly all the most prominent writers of the day were
in personal intercourse with him, and were in receipt of
pensions or gratuities from his purse. The two greatest
prose writers, Voiture and Balzac, repaid his liberality
by eulogising his administration in terms of equal
warmth and sincerity. It is true that the patronage of
an absolute ruler, whether king or minister, is not
always an unmixed benefit to literature, and that
none of Richelieu's *protégés*, except Corneille, can be
placed in the highest rank. But on the other hand
court patronage in France did effect a very notable
literary revival, and it is impossible to deny to Richelieu
some credit for the rise of the next generation of
authors, whose works have reflected such glory upon
the France of Louis XIV.

In connection with literature Richelieu will always be best remembered as the founder of the French Academy. This had its origin in the private meetings of a number of literary friends, who in 1629 formed the habit of assembling once a week for the discussion of literary topics and the consideration of each other's productions. These meetings had already been going on for four years when Richelieu was informed of them by one of the numerous busybodies whose function it was to tell him of everything that was going on in Paris. With characteristic keenness, though foreign affairs seemed sufficiently critical to absorb all his energies, he grasped the possible uses of such an organisation, and offered the members a constitution under government patronage. There was some natural hesitation, as party spirit ran high in France, and men of letters were by no means unanimously cardinalist. But the offer could not be safely or courteously refused, and letters-patent were drawn up in 1635, though the bigoted opposition of the parliament, ever jealous of new corporations, delayed their formal promulgation till July 10, 1637. The primary function of the Academy was to regulate and purify the French language, to make it the most perfect of modern tongues, and to " render it not only elegant, but also capable of treating all the arts and all the sciences." But from the first both the founder's intentions and the habits of the members combined to give it a second function as a tribunal of literary criticism. Richelieu himself pointed clearly to this duty by demanding in 1637 a corporate opinion on Corneille's *Cid*, which had been attacked

in the *Observations* of Scudéry. From this time it
became a regular part of the Academy's business to
criticise, and, if it thought fit, to express formal
approbation of the works both of members and others;
and it needs only a superficial knowledge of French
literature to appreciate what an immense influence it
has thus exerted both upon language and style.

From the political point of view the origin of
French journalism is even more important than the
foundation of the Academy, and to this also Richelieu
gave the deciding impulse. Hitherto the only newspaper in France had been an annual publication, the
Mercure françois, which was a continuation of the
Chronologie septénaire of Palma Cayet. This was
obviously insufficient to satisfy the growing interest
in political events, and it was supplemented by a
number of unauthorised fly-sheets, called *nouvelles à
la main*, which were circulated either in print or
manuscript, and eagerly read. The most industrious
compiler of news was a prominent physician,
Théophraste Renaudot, who supplied *nouvelles* for the
distraction as well as medicines for the cure of his
wealthy patients. Renaudot succeeded in gaining the
confidence of Richelieu, and in 1631 received a formal
license to transform his fugitive fly-sheets into a
regular newspaper under government sanction. Thus
was founded the *Gazette*, or, as it was called later, the
Gazette de la France. It appeared weekly in a small
quarto sheet of four pages, each containing a single
column. From the first the extent and accuracy of
its intelligence gave it a secure pre-eminence over any
rival publication, and its circulation and importance

rapidly increased. Both king and minister were among the contributors to its pages, and Louis XIII. took a special pleasure in the labour of composition and revision. Secure of this novel method of influencing opinion, Richelieu was able to dispense for the rest of his ministry with the more cumbrous system of assembling Notables which he had adopted at starting. In the words of Henri Martin, he had "given birth to the two great enemies, whose struggle was to fill the modern world—absolutism and the press."

CHAPTER IX

RICHELIEU AND THE CHURCH

Condition of the French Church during the religious wars—
Religious revival in the seventeenth century—Charitable
orders—Advance of clerical and secular education—Monastic
reform—Richelieu's relations with the papacy—Relations of
Church and State—Clerical taxation—Richelieu and St.
Cyran—Richelieu's opportunism in ecclesiastical matters—
His superstition—Case of Urbain Grandier.

RICHELIEU, although a bishop and a cardinal, was not
a great theologian, nor was he in the narrowest sense
a great churchman. Many of his contemporaries,
endowed with far less dignity and authority, yet
exercised an incomparably more distinct and vital
influence on the religious life of his time than he
can claim to have done. Still his career is coincident
with a very important epoch in the history of the
French Church, and both in his actions and in his
Memoirs he shows a very keen interest in ecclesiastical
matters, and a very vivid sense of their importance
to the order and wellbeing of the state. Possibly
his interest was rather that of the politician than of
the ecclesiastic, but it was none the less real, nor
was the influence which he could not fail to possess
diminished because he himself was lacking in spiritual

insight or because his motives were rather secular
than religious. These considerations make it impossible, even in a brief sketch like the present, to
dismiss his relations with the Church in a brief and
perfunctory paragraph.

The sixteenth century had witnessed two of the
greatest religious movements in history. The first
was the Reformation, by which a number of states,
mostly in Northern Europe, threw off all dependence
upon Rome, and adopted religious doctrines and
organisation more or less at variance with those
which had hitherto prevailed throughout Western
Christendom. By the second or Counter Reformation,
the Roman Catholic Church profited by the lessons
it had received, reformed the abuses which had
provoked discontent and rebellion, and strengthened
its internal organisation in order not only to prevent
further defections, but also to recover some of the
ground that had been lost. This reforming movement, which was immensely stimulated by the efforts
of the Jesuit order, found its final expression in the
decrees of the Council of Trent. But although France
was represented at Trent, and although the doctrinal
definitions of the council were welcomed, yet those
decrees which touched the constitution of the Church
and restored discipline were never accepted or pro-
mulgated in France. There were two primary
motives for this repudiation of the chief measures of
reform. The crown contended that the conciliar
decrees diminished the authority and patronage
conferred upon the kings by the Concordat of 1516.
The Parliament of Paris complained that they would

destroy the liberties of the Gallican Church, which
had always been dear to the official classes since their
first definition in the Pragmatic Sanction of Bourges
in 1438.

Thus the Church of France remained unreformed,
and during the religious wars the abuses of the old
system become still more numerous and conspicuous.
Many archbishoprics and bishoprics were allowed to remain vacant, while others were held by men who had
obtained them by uncanonical or simoniacal means. Most
of the bishops were non-resident and neglected their
dioceses. Du Vair, who lived at Aix as first president
of the Parliament of Provence, was bishop of Lisieux,
in Normandy, which he never visited. It is recorded
that on one occasion the bishop of St. Malo confirmed
two thousand persons in a single village, which proves
that his visits cannot have been very frequent. There
were no schools for the education of the clergy, most
of whom were extremely ignorant and incompetent.
While the revenues of the church were very large, the
village *curés* were lamentably ill-paid, and their mode
of life was practically that of the peasants from whom
they were sprung, and whom they were vainly expected
to elevate and instruct. The fabric of the churches
was in a lamentable state. Many had been used as
fortresses in the war, with very natural results; others
had been profaned or destroyed by the Huguenots. In
many parishes divine service had come to an end
altogether, and the people were left without any religious
ministrations. And if the condition of the secular
clergy was bad, that of the regulars was still worse.
The headships of religious houses were frequently given

to children or to persons of scandalous character. In many cases the abbot was a layman, who drew the revenues of the monastery, while his duties were discharged by an ill-paid substitute. The count of Soissons was said to receive an ecclesiastical revenue of 100,000 livres a year, while his place was filled by a prior with an annual income of 1000. Elsewhere the revenues, both of monasteries and of bishoprics, were saddled with pensions and reserves which had been granted to courtiers of both sexes. Discipline was completely neglected, and both monks and nuns lived worldly, self-indulgent, and often vicious lives.

The termination of the religious wars by the accession of Henry IV. and his acceptance of the Roman Catholic faith was followed by a notable religious revival in France, which reached its zenith during Richelieu's ministry. But this revival was not the work of the state, nor even of the Church acting in its corporate capacity. The whole credit belongs to a few devoted and highly-gifted individuals, whose lives will always attract attention and admiration as long as the record of religious enthusiasm and heroic self-sacrifice awakens any responsive chord in the hearts of mankind. The dominant impulse was given by a native of Savoy, St. François de Sales, but the most active and influential worker was a Frenchman, the famous St. Vincent de Paul. As was natural, the revival was a composite and many-sided movement. One of its manifestations was a general desire among the clergy to strengthen the bonds which connected France with the Universal Church, of which she professed to be the eldest daughter. This Ultramontane tendency was specially encouraged

by the Jesuits, who had been restored to France in
1604 after a brief period of exile, and at once gained
great influence at court by supplying a series of royal
confessors. Another sign of the revival was the endeavour of the Church to free itself from the trammels
of state control, to recover as much as possible the free
election of its own dignitaries, and, above all, to restore
the independence of clerical judicature, which had been
much restricted by the encroachments of the secular courts,
and especially by the practice of appealing on purely
clerical matters from the Church courts to the Parliament of Paris (the famous *appel comme d'abus*). But by
far the most conspicuous and creditable aspect of the
movement was its practical side, the immense energy
and enthusiasm that was thrown into the work of
active charity, of education, and of monastic reform.

The Roman Catholic Church has always shown itself
honourably conscious of its duties towards the poor and
afflicted, but at no time and place has it undertaken the
task of charitable relief with more devotion than in the
early part of the seventeenth century. It was upon
pious women that the task was mainly thrown, and
among the numerous orders that were founded to
systematise and encourage their labours two are
specially conspicuous for the piety of their founders
and for their subsequent development. The Visitandines,
or Congregation of the Visitation, were founded at
Annecy by François de Sales, and a branch was
established in Paris in 1621 by Madame de Chantal.
In the eighteenth century the order possessed more than
a hundred houses in France. Still more famous and
useful have been the *Sœurs de la Charité*, or Gray

Sisters, founded and organised by Vincent de Paul in 1633, and rapidly extended under the headship of Madame Legras. This organisation—for it can hardly be called an order—was mainly composed of women of humble origin, whose habits and training fitted them for the toilsome and often repulsive labours which they undertook. At the same time Vincent de Paul succeeded in enlisting in the good work many ladies of the highest rank, who, with the title of *Dames de la Charité*, undertook the task of organising relief, and acting as visitors and overseers of the humbler Sisters. So great was their success, according to an admiring biographer of the founder, that in the first year of their activity no less than 760 heretics were converted to the orthodox faith. Prominent among these ladies was Richelieu's favourite niece, Madame de Combalet, afterwards duchess d'Aiguillon, and it was she who succeeded in enlisting her uncle's sympathy and support in a work which he probably thought outside the duties of the state, and which he had little time or inclination to direct in person.

Almost equally numerous were the associations formed for the education and training of the clergy. Here the lead was taken by de Bérulle, who founded the *Oratoire de Jésus* in 1611, and obtained its approval from Paul V. in 1613. Within a brief period the Oratorians possessed no less than fifty houses, and among their pupils were such men as Malebranche, Mascaron, and Massillon. De Bérulle found numerous imitators, of whom the chief were Adrien Bourdoise, the founder of the seminary of St. Nicolas du Chardonnet, and Jean Jacques Olier, who organised in

1641 the celebrated seminary of St. Sulpice. But in the work of clerical education, as in that of charity, by far the most successful and practical organiser was Vincent de Paul. The Congregation of the Mission was founded by him in 1625 in the Collège des Bons Enfants, and in 1632, when it received formal confirmation from Urban VIII., was moved into more spacious quarters in the Priory of St. Lazare, whence its members obtained the name of *Lazaristes*. The success of this institution in raising the standard of piety and priestly activity throughout the country districts was marvellous, and attracted the interested attention of Richelieu. In an interview with Vincent de Paul he asked for full information as to the aims and constitution of the order, and gave it solid encouragement by recommending its more prominent members for ecclesiastical promotion.

Nor was the work of secular education neglected in the general revival of clerical enthusiasm. The Congregation of the Ursulines, founded in Italy in the previous century, was now introduced into France by Madeleine Lhuillier, and devoted itself with marked success to the teaching of girls. But by far the greatest educating force was supplied by the Jesuits. The edict for their restoration in 1604 allowed them to possess thirteen colleges in the provinces, but they were at first excluded from the capital. This obstacle was overcome by the influence of the king's confessor, Father Cotton, and in 1609 they were permitted to give public instruction in the Collège de Clermont. This gave rise to a long and bitter struggle between the Jesuits and the University of Paris, in which the former only held their own

through the unwavering support of Richelieu. He had
little sympathy with the Jesuits, who were opposed
both to his foreign policy and to much of his home
government, but he realised that in education, if not
in commerce, a monopoly is a dangerous gift to a
corporation. Thanks to his support, the pupils of the
Order in 1627 numbered no fewer than 13,195. This
strenuous competition was wholesome to the University
itself, which at last abandoned the effort to suppress its
rivals, and set to work to recover its declining influence
by improving its own methods of instruction.

If Richelieu's attitude towards the work of charity
and education was passive rather than active, he took a
more direct interest in the furtherance of monastic
reform. This holds a prominent place among the
proposals which he submitted to the king in 1625, and
throughout his ministry he endeavoured by frequent
visitations to enforce the observance of the stricter
rules of monastic life. To increase his authority for
this purpose he obtained his own nomination as general
of the great orders of Cluny, Citeaux, and the Premon-
stratensians, in spite of the opposition of the pope, who
refused to confirm him in the two latter offices. But
the magistrates and other secular agents whom Richelieu
employed provoked ecclesiastical jealousy and opposition,
and in the end a great deal more was effected by
individual initiative than by government intervention.
By far the greatest achievements of the period were
the foundation of the reformed Benedictine Congregation of St. Maur, whence proceeded in the next
generation the monumental works of French erudition,
and the restoration of discipline in the nunneries of

Port Royal and Maubuisson by the famous Angelique
Arnauld. From Port Royal nuns were despatched on
missions to extend the work of reform to all the
convents of France. But if Richelieu's share in the
movement was less predominant than he probably
anticipated, yet his example and patronage contributed
to the success of the efforts of others, and he may
further claim the credit of having terminated the long
warfare between regulars and seculars. By the decision
of a conference which he initiated, and whose labours he
personally superintended, the jealousy with which the
parish priests had always regarded the intervention of
their rivals was at last allayed. The monks were
subjected to episcopal authority, and they were only
allowed to preach and receive confession with the
express permission of the ordinary.

So far the ecclesiastical revival had proceeded with
Richelieu's approval, and to some extent with his active
encouragement and support. But with the Ultramontane
tendencies of the movement he came into direct and
hostile collision. During the minority of Louis XIII.
the support of Mary de Medici had enabled cardinal
du Perron and the Ultramontane party in France to
gain a considerable increase of strength. This was
conclusively proved by the removal of Richer, the chief
champion of Gallican liberties, from his office of Syndic
in the Sorbonne, by the frustration of the Parliament's
attack on the Jesuits, and by the attitude assumed by
the clerical estate in the States-General. But this
progress was checked by the accession of Richelieu to
power. With his strong sense of the overpowering
importance of national interests, he was not likely to be

submissive to a foreign authority, whose action could
not possibly be dictated by a single-minded regard for
France. Among his early measures the expulsion of
papal troops from the Valtelline and the conclusion
of the treaty of 1626 with the Huguenots excited
the horrified animosity of the Roman Catholic world.
Bitter attacks were published against the "cardinal of
the Huguenots," the betrayer of his Church to the
infidels, and Richelieu thought it necessary to procure a
condemnation of these libels from a clerical synod. It
was at this juncture that a book reached Paris from
Rome, written by a Jesuit, Sanctarellus, and approved
both by the pope and the General of the Order. In
this book, "the most evil of its kind," as Richelieu calls
it, were maintained in their most extreme form the
doctrines of papal absolutism : "the pope may punish
and depose kings, not only for heresy and schism, but
for any intolerable offence, for incapacity or for negli-
gence ; he has power to admonish kings and to punish
them with death ; all princes who govern states do so
by commission from His Holiness, who may claim to
govern them himself, etc." These maxims, says Richelieu,
are capable of ruining the whole Church, and they are
the more preposterous with regard to the pope, as he
"is a temporal prince, and has made no such renunciation of earthly greatness as to be indifferent to it." He
hastened to stimulate the Gallican sentiment in opposition to such teaching. The Sorbonne, or theological
faculty of the University, censured the book as "containing novel, false, and erroneous doctrines, contrary to
the word of God, and rendering odious the dignity of
the sovereign Pontiff." The parliament ordered the

book to be publicly burned, and eagerly seized the
opportunity to renew their attack upon the Jesuits,
whom they proposed to expel from their colleges, and
even from France. Richelieu, however, interfered to
check their ardour, in the belief that "it was necessary to reduce the Jesuits to such a state that they
had no power to be harmful, but not to drive them to
attempt any mischief from despair." The Order escaped
further persecution by accepting a solemn declaration
that they repudiated the doctrines of Sanctarellus about
the power of kings, that they acknowledged that kings
hold immediately of God, and that they would never
teach any doctrines on this matter other than those held
by the clergy, the Universities of the kingdom, and the
Sorbonne.

This alliance of Richelieu with the Gallican party
could not but be distasteful to the papal court, and it
was by no means obliterated by subsequent services,
such as the taking of La Rochelle, and the strengthening
of the temporal power of the papacy by the anti-Spanish
policy pursued in the Mantuan succession. On the
strength of these services Richelieu ventured to demand
a boon for which he was extremely eager—that he should
be appointed papal legate in France, as cardinal Amboise
had been in the reign of Louis XII. But Urban VIII.
had no mind to give increased power to a prelate who
was already sufficiently independent, and it is possible
that Richelieu's leniency to the Huguenots was in some
measure a retaliation for this refusal. Nor were his
other requests more favourably received. Urban refused
to make him legate in Avignon, to allow his nomination
as coadjutor of the archbishop of Trier, and to confirm

him as general of the three great monastic orders. The
cardinal's hat was never granted to Father Joseph, in
spite of the persistent efforts of the French government; and the pope steadfastly declined to recognise
the validity of the decision which pronounced the
marriage of Gaston with Margaret of Lorraine to be
null and void.

These continued rebuffs, and especially the last,
inspired Richelieu with the wish to teach the pope a
lesson. Pierre Dupuy, one of the ablest of the authors
whose learning was always at the cardinal's command,
drew up an exhaustive treatise on the *Libertés de l'Eglise
Gallicane*, which stated fully the arguments not only
against papal despotism, but also for the subjection of
the church to the state. This book, which was published
anonymously in 1638, caused the greatest sensation
both in France and at Rome, and the council found it
advisable to decree its suppression, though only on the
technical ground that it had been published without
license. But the book continued to be sold, and in the
next year the execution of an attendant of the French
envoy at Rome gave rise to an open quarrel. The
envoy, d'Estrées, ceased all communications with the
Vatican. Louis XIII. closed his doors to the papal
nuncio in Paris, and forbade the bishops to hold any
intercourse with him. It was currently reported that
Richelieu was prepared to break off all connection with
Rome and to obtain from a national synod his own
election as patriarch of France. A priest named Hersent
hastened to denounce the projected schism in a treatise
which he published under the title of *Optatus Gallus.*
The bishops did not venture to defend the book, and

the parliament hastened to proscribe it, and indirectly to
express approval of the doctrines of Dupuy.   But the
pope could not afford to carry any further his quarrel
with France.   Satisfaction was given to d'Estrées, and
the grant of a cardinal's hat to Mazarin, who acted as
papal envoy on the occasion, was taken as the pledge of
reconciliation.   But Urban VIII. never forgave the
prelate who had humbled him.   On Richelieu's death he
refused to allow the usual commemorative service for a
cardinal to be celebrated at Rome, and he is said to
have expressed his opinion of the dead statesman's
character in terms which sound oddly in the mouth
of a pope: "If there is a God, he will pay dearly for
his conduct; but if there is no God, then he was truly
an admirable man."

Although Richelieu was the champion of Gallican
liberties against papal pretensions, he was equally
resolute to enforce the duties of the clergy to the state.
In this respect his conduct as a minister stands in
instructive contrast to the more purely clerical attitude
which he had assumed at the meeting of the States-
General.   In his speech as orator of the clergy he had
made the following claims for his order: (1) the more
frequent admission of ecclesiastics to office and to the
royal council; (2) the prohibition of future grants of
church revenues to laymen, either directly or by way of
pensions and reserves; (3) the release of the clergy from
direct taxes, on the ground that the only tribute which
they owed was their prayers; (4) the restoration of
clerical jurisdiction to its former limits and independence;
(5) the recognition of the decrees of the Council of Trent.
Of these demands the only one which he gratified when

the opportunity came was the first. His partiality for
ecclesiastical agents, not only in diplomacy, but in
military and naval commands, was a subject of derision
in Europe, and gave a handle against him to the pope,
who openly expressed his disapproval of the employment
of churchmen, like the cardinal de la Valette, in leading
armies to the field. The other proposals proved nothing
more than pious wishes. The Council of Trent remained unacknowledged. The diversion of ecclesiastical revenues to laymen continued, and Richelieu himself
is said to have rewarded a favourite fiddler with the gift
of an abbey. No limit was placed on the encroachment
of the secular courts on church jurisdiction, nor on
the employment of the *appel comme d'abus*. And the
question of clerical taxation gave rise to an open and
envenomed quarrel between Richelieu and his fellow-
clergy.

The revenues of the French clergy, whether from
land or from other sources, were wholly exempt from
direct taxation. The clerical assemblies were in the
habit of making an annual grant of 2,000,000 livres,
but they always protested that this was a *don gratuit*
and not a compulsory payment, and, moreover, such a
sum was ludicrously out of proportion to the wealth of
the Church. Among the financial expedients forced
upon Richelieu by military expenses were increased
demands on the liberality of the Church synods, and
these were usually granted, though always with
murmuring and reluctance. But in 1640 he came
forward with a wholly novel and unforeseen demand.
His supporter and confidant, the bishop of Chartres,
had collected documents from the royal archives to

prove that land could only be held in mortmain by
letters-patent, to be obtained on payment of a *droit
d'amortissement*. This form the clergy had systematically
failed to observe, and therefore it was held that their
lands were legally forfeited to the crown. Instead of
enforcing this claim, it was determined to collect all
arrears of payment due since the year 1520, when
Francis I. had levied a similar exaction. The sum thus
due was estimated at nearly 80,000,000 livres, but the
government announced that it would be content with
3,600,000. The clergy were furious at the attempt to
collect such a payment without consulting their assembly.
It was at this time that the quarrel with Rome was at
its height, and that Hersent published his *Optatus Gallus*,
which attacked Richelieu's conduct at home as well as
his attitude towards the papacy. Regardless of this
opposition, the council issued an edict in October 1640,
demanding the additional payment of one-sixth of church
revenues for two years. But the clergy, encouraged by
the prospect of papal aid, prepared for strenuous
resistance to the "tyrant" and "apostate" who so shame-
lessly violated the privileges of his own order. Richelieu,
unwilling to face this domestic storm at a time when
foreign affairs demanded all his attention, found it
advisable to give way to some extent, and agreed to
summon an assembly of the clergy. The assembly met
at Mantes early in 1641, and it was announced that all
the claims of the government would be commuted for a
lump sum of 6,600,000 livres. Even this diminished
demand provoked a storm of indignation. The archbishop of Sens recalled the ancient maxim that "the
people contribute their goods, the nobles their blood,

and the clergy their prayers," and declared that the liberty of the Church would be destroyed if "they were compelled to open their hands instead of their lips." Montchal, archbishop of Toulouse, whose *Memoirs* give the most vivid picture of the passions that were excited on the subject, termed the royal exactions "a horrible sacrilege committed on the property of the cross," and declared "our kings have always believed that the gold of the sanctuary would be fatal to them unless they received it as a gift." Richelieu found it necessary to take violent measures, and the two archbishops, with four other bishops, were ordered to quit Mantes and retire to their respective dioceses, without venturing to pass through Paris on the way. Their withdrawal enabled the dispute to be compromised. The majority agreed to pay a sum of five millions and a half, with which the government professed itself satisfied, and this settlement was followed by the reconciliation with the papacy.

The same determination to prevent Gallicanism from developing into a claim for clerical independence, and to enforce at all hazards the solidarity and authority of the state, is visible in Richelieu's relations with one of his most famous contemporaries, the Abbé de St. Cyran. St. Cyran had not yet become the founder of a sect, but he was already famous as the reputed author of *Petrus Aurelius*, and as a formidable free-lance on the side of Gallican liberties. His piety and learning gave him an influence quite out of proportion to his ecclesiastical rank : he was the spiritual director of Port Royal, which had been transferred by Angelique Arnauld to Paris, and he was the confidential adviser of many

distinguished persons of both sexes.. St. Cyran's concep-
tion of the Church as an oligarchy of bishops rather
than a monarchy brought him into collision with Rome,
and both he and his friend Jansen had been from the
first hostile critics of the principles and morality of
Jesuit teaching. Both these positions commended
themselves to Richelieu, who was engaged in a quarrel
with the papacy, and had good reason to dislike the
Ultramontane and Spanish predilections of the Jesuits.
In his early days he had been brought into intimate
relations with St. Cyran, through their common friend
the bishop of Poitiers, and he now made strenuous
efforts to gain the allegiance of the man whom he
openly declared to be the most learned theologian in
Europe. No less than five bishoprics—some say eight
—were successively offered to the friend of his youth.
But St. Cyran resolutely refused to sacrifice his independence by accepting preferment from a "government
which only wished for slaves." The autocracy, which
he suspected Richelieu of a desire to establish, was
quite as repugnant to his principles as the absolutism of
the pope. His obstinate self-confidence and isolation
were the first cause of Richelieu's enmity. The higher
his appreciation of St. Cyran's ability, the more he
mistrusted the growth of an influence which was outside
his control. And to this first ground of alienation others
were speedily added. We have seen what importance
Richelieu attached to the dissolution of Gaston's marriage
with Margaret of Lorraine. On this subject St. Cyran
did not hesitate to take the same line as Urban VIII.,
and to declare that it was impious to annul a sacrament
of the Church for purely political reasons. But probably

the greatest displeasure was caused by the action of
Jansen, of whose teaching St. Cyran was already the
avowed champion.   Jansen, a native of the Spanish
Netherlands, had published the *Mars Gallicus*, in which
he bitterly denounced the conduct of France in betraying the cause of Roman Catholicism by an open alliance
with Lutherans and Calvinists.   This pamphlet, which
earned from the Spanish government the elevation of
its author to the bishopric of Ypres, appeared in a
French translation in 1638.   Richelieu was always
keenly sensitive to such attacks on his policy, and as he
could not touch the chief culprit, he determined to take
vengeance on the disciple.   In May 1638 St. Cyran
was arrested and imprisoned in Vincennes, where he
remained till the cardinal's death.   His papers were
seized, and a judicial inquiry instituted, in the hope of
obtaining evidence for a charge of heresy, but the scheme
resulted in failure, and the prisoner was never brought
to trial.   That Richelieu foresaw the formation of a
Jansenist sect as the inevitable result of St. Cyran's
combination of personal independence with deep spiritual
influence over others is proved by his comparing him
with the great reformers of the previous century.   "If
Luther and Calvin," he said, "had been imprisoned
when they began to dogmatise, the states of Europe
would have been spared many troubles."   Later, when
the prince of Condé tried to obtain the prisoner's
release, he replied, "Do you know the man you are
speaking of? he is more dangerous than six armies."
But the cardinal's harshness towards an innocent opponent was subtly avenged by the famous John of
Werth.   He had been a captive since the battle of

Rheinfelden, and had made St. Cyran's acquaintance in
their common prison of Vincennes. The general was
brought from his confinement to witness the sumptuous
representation of Richelieu's comedy of *Miriame* before
the king and court. When asked for his opinion of
the spectacle, he replied that it was magnificent, but
that what astounded him most was to find " in the
Most Christian kingdom, the bishops at the comedy and
the saints in prison." Richelieu pretended not to hear,
but the blow must have struck shrewdly home.

It is impossible to discover in Richelieu's relations with
the Church any signs that he was actuated by profound
convictions or overmastering principles. Though he
made use of parties, he belonged to none. In ecclesiastical matters, as contrasted with politics, he was an
opportunist pure and simple. If the pope had not
refused his demands, and tried to thwart his schemes,
he would never have identified himself with the advocates
of Gallicanism. So long as Gallican liberties existed in
practice he had no desire that they should be defined
or formally recognised. When an open quarrel with
Rome broke out, his haughty and stubborn temper
doubtless prompted him to carry it through after the
fashion of Henry VIII., and to establish the patriarch-
ate which his enemies accused him of coveting. But
his temper rarely got the better of his discretion. He
was keen-sighted enough to apprehend the differences,
both of history and opinion, which rendered the action
of England no safe guide for France, and he foresaw
that a final rupture with the papacy would produce
such a ferment that the political influence of his country
would be annihilated for at least half a century. Again,

he was far too thoroughly imbued with the spirit of his
order to be a consistent and thoroughgoing Erastian.
If the clergy had not been always suspicious of his
Protestant alliances, and often sympathetic with the
enemies of France, he would never have stirred a step
from his way to attack their corporate privileges and
independence.

It was this detachment from religious partisan-
ship which enabled him to subordinate ecclesiastical to
political considerations, and to be the first European
statesman who ventured to translate the principles of
toleration into practice.   His attitude in this respect
is the more remarkable when we remember that he
was no eighteenth century sceptic, confident in human
powers and doubtful of divine intervention.   If Richelieu
profoundly·influenced his age, it was not because he was
before it, but because he so thoroughly identified himself
with it.   It would be misleading to call him a religious
man, but he was certainly superstitious.   His private
letters furnish plentiful evidence of his belief in astrology,
in magic, and in the small popular prejudices against
unlucky days and actions.   This vein of superstition—
not uncommon in great men of action—merits the more
attention, because without it it would be impossible
to plead any defence for Richelieu in an episode which
looms very largely in the pages of his detractors—the
case of Urbain Grandier.   The story itself is sufficiently remarkable, and though the evidence has now
been fully published, there are several questions connected with the case which it is difficult to answer
with absolute certainty.

Urbain Grandier was a priest of Loudun in Poitou,

of a handsome and imposing exterior, and possessed of
great influence over women, which he almost certainly
abused. In one way and another he had excited the
enmity of several prominent inhabitants of the town,
who brought against him a charge of immorality and
impiety. In the court of the bishop of Poitiers he was
condemned, but on appeal the sentence was reversed
both by the *présidial* of Poitiers and by the archbishop
of Bordeaux. Grandier's too obvious exultation in his
triumph redoubled the fury of his opponents, who were
eager to find some new means of procuring his ruin.
One of them, Mignon, was director of the Ursuline
convent in Loudun. Rumours began to spread that
some of the nuns were possessed with devils, that they
were afflicted with extraordinary bodily contortions, and
that in their ravings they brought grave charges against
Grandier. The director and other priests were called in
to exorcise the demons, and they reported that they
obtained from the mouths of the latter a reluctant confession as to the master who had sent them. Still no
formal charge was brought, and opinion in Loudun was
divided between Grandier's accusers and defenders. As
before, the bishop of Poitiers was on one side, professed
his belief in the evidence, while the archbishop of Bordeaux was incredulous. It was at this juncture that a
commissioner of the government, Laubardemont, came
to Loudun to superintend the destruction of the castle.
He was a confidential agent of Richelieu, and was sub-
sequently employed to collect evidence against St. Cyran.
The popularity of a professed spy and informer was not
likely to be great, and his reputation has consequently
suffered. Laubardemont was completely gained over by

the stories of Grandier's accusers.   He undertook to
bring the whole matter before the cardinal, and he is
said to have prejudiced him against the accused by
asserting that Grandier was the author of a scurrilous
libel, *Le Cordonnier de Loudun*, that had been circulated
when Richelieu was a resident in Poitou as bishop of
Luçon.   The result was that a special commission of
fourteen persons, with Laubardemont at its head, was
appointed to try the case.   The trial itself was, from a
modern point of view, farcical, the bias of the court was
unmistakable, and the evidence was mainly that which
the exorcists professed to have extracted from the so-
called devils.   Grandier was sentenced to death, tortured
to make him confess his accomplices, and finally burned
under circumstances of exceptional and wanton bar-
barity.

That Grandier's death was a judicial murder of the
worst kind, and that fraud as well as credulity entered
into the conduct of the case against him, is incontestable.
But it is by no means easy to distribute equally the
exact measures of guilt.   That the whole affair was a
gigantic conspiracy, in which nuns, priests, the bishop
of Poitiers, and many others played preconcerted parts
to destroy a common enemy, is preposterous.   The very
length of time—two years—during which the professed
marvels were prolonged is conclusive against such extensive and well-organised complicity.   The further
assertion of Gui Patin that Richelieu was at the bottom
of the plot, and that he resorted to such an elaborate
imposture to ruin a humble but detested libeller, is not
only absurd in itself, but runs counter to all that we
know of the cardinal's open, if often excessive, malevo-

lence. The probability is that the nuns suffered from religious hysteria, of which there are many recorded instances in the same period of revival, and that the suggestions of their spiritual director led them to make their incoherent charges against the priest whom he was known to detest, and of whom they had doubtless heard much that was evil. Some, at any rate, of the exorcists were men whose character raises them above the charge of deliberate ill-faith. All that can be urged against Richelieu is that he saw no *a priori* difficulties as to the credibility of the accusations, and that he allowed the machinery of a special commission, always more likely to look for guilt than for innocence, to be employed in a case where there was no possible justification for its use.

CHAPTER X

RICHELIEU'S LAST YEARS

1641-1642

RICHELIEU did not live to witness the conclusion of the
great war in which France had engaged under his auspices.
The treaties of Westphalia and the Pyrenees, especially
the latter, might have been concluded earlier if his life had
been prolonged, but in spite of the delay he is as much
their author as if he had signed the actual documents. In
fact, all the substantial advantages which France gained
by these treaties had been practically secured by 1640.
The military events of the next two years did little but
render more certain the ultimate triumph of France.
In 1641 the flowing tide of French successes seemed for
a moment to be arrested. In Italy and in Artois the
French troops had enough to do to hold their own.

Charles of Lorraine was restored, only to prove once more a traitor to his promises, and his duchy had to be re-occupied before the year was over. In Germany Guébriant defeated the Imperialists at Wolfenbüttel, but the death of Baner and other causes prevented the allies from gaining any important results by their success. In 1642, however, the French cause made rapid and decisive strides. In Italy the princes Thomas and Maurice deserted the Spaniards to join their sister-in-law, and their adhesion turned the balance decisively in favour of the French. A great effort was planned by Richelieu on the side of the Pyrenees, and the capture of Perpignan and Salces completed the second and final union of Roussillon to France. In Germany Guébriant opened the year with a decisive victory at Kempten, and this was followed by a campaign in which Torstenson, Baner's successor, emulated the most brilliant achievements of Gustavus Adolphus. By a series of rapid and masterly movements this general, though imprisoned in his litter by gout, overran Silesia and Moravia, and caused a panic in Vienna. Compelled to retreat by superior forces, he threw himself into Saxony and laid siege to Leipzig. When the Imperialists advanced to relieve the city, he crushed them on the plain of Breitenfeld (Nov. 2, 1642), where Gustavus Adolphus, eleven years before, had won the first great victory which established his own reputation and marked a decisive turning-point in the history of the war. The surrender of Leipzig was the reward of Torstenson's success, and the news of this brilliant triumph must have brought some consolation to Richelieu as he lay on his death-bed.

The enemies of France did not require the lessons of 1642 to teach them that little hope remained for them in arms. They had already realised that their only chance of recovering from their reverses lay in the overthrow by domestic treason of the minister whom they regarded as the author of all their misfortunes. In spite of the glory which his administration had brought to France, Richelieu had still many enemies who longed for his overthrow, and few adherents who would make strenuous efforts for his defence. Probably his best friend — though few suspected it, and perhaps the cardinal himself as little as the general public—was the king. The private letters of Louis XIII., in these two years, prove that he was not devoid of gratitude and even affection towards the man who had made his reign illustrious, though the coldness of his manner and a certain peevish resentment of anything like dictation misled even those in his most immediate confidence into a belief that it was no impossible task to alienate the king from the minister. Richelieu had ever to be on his guard against secret foes at court, who were far more dangerous than his avowed opponents. Among the latter the most prominent was the count of Soissons, who had never forgiven his defeat of 1636. He had been living ever since in the border fortress of Sedan, whence he carried on incessant intrigues with foreign states, with malcontents at home, and with the nobles who had followed the queen-mother into exile. In 1641 the young duke of Guise arrived in Sedan, and discussed with Soissons and Bouillon, the governor of the fortress, the organisation of an armed rebellion for Richelieu's overthrow. The cardinal, informed of their projects, sent orders to Bouillon to withdraw his hospitality from Soissons, and to the latter to depart for Venice. This message was the signal for civil war. The conspirators threw off all disguise and applied for aid to Spain and Austria, who were only too glad to encourage a movement which could not fail to serve their ends. The king on his side declared Soissons, Guise, and Bouillon enemies of the state, and despatched the marshal de Châtillon to combine with the restored duke of Lorraine in an attack on Sedan. But Charles of Lorraine had already decided to break his recent treaty with France, and Châtillon was forced to stand on the defensive against the rebels, who received the aid of an Imperialist detachment under Lamboy. Their forces had already quitted Sedan and crossed the Meuse when they were attacked by the royal troops at La Marfée. It was generally anticipated that the first conflict would have decisive results, and that a victory of the insurgents would be followed by a movement on the part of Richelieu's opponents at the court and in Paris. But good fortune was on the cardinal's side, and the forecast, shrewd as it was, proved fallacious. No victory could have been more decisive. The royalist cavalry had been tampered with, and the infantry, left to itself, fled in panic-stricken confusion. But in the turmoil Soissons was killed by a chance bullet, and the death of the rebel leader, whose rank as a prince of the blood made him indispensable, deprived his confederates of all the fruits of their success. The whole scheme of rebellion was at an end. Guise fled to Brussels, Bouillon submitted and was pardoned, and their secret sympathisers at court had to wait for a more favourable opportunity, only too pleased that they had not betrayed themselves by a premature movement.

Gratitude, as Richelieu had good reason to know, is rarely a permanent force in politics, and the most active and resolute of his opponents at court was a young man who owed his advancement entirely to the cardinal. Henri d'Effiat, marquis de Cinq-Mars, was the son of the marquis d'Effiat, who had been for four years super-intendent of finance, but had won more renown as a military leader. Richelieu had brought Cinq-Mars to the notice of Louis XIII. at a moment when he wished to divert the king's interest from the society of Made-moiselle d'Hautefort, to whom Louis's platonic affections had returned after the retirement of Louise de la Fayette. The move was successful in gaining its immediate end. Good looks and an attractive manner gained for Cinq-Mars the favour of the king, and he was speedily advanced to the office of grand equerry. But this rapid promotion turned his head. The pleasures and magnificence of the court failed to satisfy him, and he aspired to the rank of duke and peer, to military distinction, and to political ascendency. Richelieu saw clearly that he must resign all hope of using Cinq-Mars as a submissive tool, and he consoled himself for his disappointment by ruthlessly snubbing his youthful ambitions. His pretensions to the hand of Marie de Gonzaga, afterwards queen of Poland, were treated as a piece of ridiculous presumption. His endeavour to remain in attendance on Louis at meetings of the council, and even at personal conferences between the king and minister, was resented as a gross impertinence. Like most young men, Cinq-Mars could endure anything better than contempt, and he became the bitter enemy of his former patron. Confident in his secure hold of the king's affection, he resolved to play the part of a Luynes, vainly hoping that Richelieu would be as easily got rid of as Concini had been.

Cinq-Mars had been an accomplice in the conspiracy of Soissons, and had been terribly frightened by its sudden collapse. But his courage returned when he found that his complicity was undiscovered, and he resumed the schemes which had been for a moment interrupted. His chief confidant was François de Thou, a son of the famous historian, who had enjoyed and then forfeited the favour of Richelieu. He seems to have been genuinely convinced that his inconstant employer was the oppressor of France and the wanton disturber of the peace of Europe. Cinq-Mars had for a time entertained the idea of assassination as the best method of removing his enemy, but de Thou, more upright if less thoroughgoing, persuaded him to abstain from crime and to adhere to the well-worn methods of conspiracy. In order to gain a refuge and a rallying point, in case armed rebellion became imperative, de Thou was sent to gain over the veteran intriguer, Bouillon, who was still in possession of the invaluable stronghold of Sedan. As a prince of the blood was deemed indispensable to serve as a figure-head for the rebels, overtures were made to Gaston of Orleans, who had been living in tranquil obscurity since the birth of a dauphin had reduced him to comparative insignificance. Bouillon, distrusting the strength of purely native effort, insisted on the necessity of foreign assistance. In spite of the opposition of de Thou, who had

unusual scruples about embarking in obvious treason,
Fontrailles, another friend of Cinq-Mars, was despatched
to procure the support of Spain, on condition that when
peace should be made after the accomplishment of the
coup d'état all French conquests in the war should be
surrendered. In the meantime no efforts were to be
spared by the favourite to detach Louis from Richelieu's
influence, and to convince the king that his own comfort, the prosperity of France, and the peace of Europe
required the cardinal's dismissal as an indispensable
condition.

On his side Richelieu, of all statesmen the best
served by his spies, was by no means blind to the
dangers which threatened him. He had made a last
effort to disarm Cinq-Mars and to remove him from the
court by offering him the government of Touraine.
The offer was refused, and from that moment there
was open war between the two men. But there was
as yet no evidence sufficient to convince Louis XIII.
of the treasonable designs of his favourite, and until
that could be obtained the struggle resolved itself into
a duel for the dominant influence over the king; and
for this the two rivals seemed to outside observers not
unequally matched.

But if they appeared equally matched in one respect,
in others the contrast was complete and striking. Cinq-
Mars was in the prime of youthful strength and beauty,
confident in his magnetic charm of manner, eager to
prove his yet untried and possibly overestimated abilities,
and proudly anticipating the brilliant future that seemed
to await him. Richelieu, on the other hand, had little
to hope from the future. He had never enjoyed real

health since his boyhood, and he was now a prematurely
old man, broken down by sixteen years of incessant
anxiety and uninterrupted labours. Louis XIII., though
a much younger man, was also in feeble heath. During
the winter his death had seemed more than possible, and
the conspirators had busied themselves with schemes
for the exclusion of the cardinal from all share in the
government during the anticipated minority. The king
had recovered, but he was never more than an invalid
again, and he was not destined to survive the cardinal
by many months. In spite of their weakness, both king
and minister set out early in 1642 to superintend in
person the military operations in Roussillon. Travelling
separately and by easy stages, they both reached Narbonne in March. There Richelieu, prostrated with
fever and tortured by an abscess in his right arm, found
that farther progress was impossible. The doctors
advised him to seek a more healthy air in Provence, and
Louis XIII., after a delay of more than a month, set out
without him to Perpignan (April 21). Richelieu's
physical sufferings were thus reinforced by the moral
agony which it caused him to part from the king at
this critical moment, and thus to leave the field clear
for the intrigues of his youthful rival. For another
month he remained at Narbonne, detained partly by
anxiety and partly by weakness. On May 3, conscious
that death was not far distant, he dictated his will to a
notary of the town. The bulk of his property he left
to his relatives, with the exception of his library, which
he bequeathed to the nation, and his residence in Paris,
the Palais-Cardinal, which he left to the king, together
with the sum of 1,500,000 livres belonging to the

public funds, but which he kept in his own hands for
use as occasion might arise.   Four days later he set out
on his painful journey to Provence.

Richelieu had reached Arles when the long-expected
weapon was placed in his hands, in the shape of a copy
of the treaty concluded by the conspirators with Spain.
How the secret was originally betrayed has never been
known.   This proof of treason he at once despatched to
Louis, who could no longer hesitate to take action.
Probably the danger on this side had never been as
great as the cardinal, in his weakness and mistrust, had
dreaded.   Louis had not for a moment dreamed of
seriously balancing the claims of the favourite and the
minister to his confidence.   He had listened to the
suggestions and accusations of Cinq-Mars because he
had always found it easier to endure than to check the
outbursts of those around him, but on more than one
occasion he had been sufficiently outspoken to betray
his real intention to any one whose perceptions were not
blinded by conceit and self-confidence.   The arrival of
Richelieu's communication only hastened a decision that
had been already formed.   On June 10 he left Perpignan
and returned to Narbonne.   Cinq-Mars might still have
escaped by a prompt flight to Sedan, but he recklessly
rushed on his fate, and determined to follow the king.
On June 12 the order was issued for the imprisonment
of Cinq-Mars and de Thou, and messengers were sent to
arrest Bouillon in the midst of the army in Italy, of
which he had lately received the command.   The king
now set out to join Richelieu at Tarascon, and on June
28 the interview took place in the cardinal's chamber.
There the king and minister, both in bed, agreed upon

the steps to be taken for the maintenance of order and
the punishment of the guilty. Two days later Louis
appointed Richelieu lieutenant-governor of the kingdom
with the full powers of royalty, and set out on his return
to Paris, having neither the strength nor the inclination
to revisit Roussillon.

The collection of evidence against the three prisoners
was not a matter of difficulty. Gaston of Orleans was
ready, as usual, to purchase his own safety by betraying his associates. He made a full confession of his
relations with Cinq-Mars and of the treaty with Spain,
pleading only that he was innocent of any plot for the
cardinal's assassination. To inflict an adequate punishment on the king's brother was impossible, but Richelieu
seized the opportunity to humiliate his ancient adversary.
Gaston was compelled to sign a full deposition for use
against his accomplices, and to renounce for the future
all claims to " any office, employment, or administration
in the kingdom." On these terms he was allowed to
reside at Blois as a private individual. Nor did
Richelieu spare the king for the encouragement which,
consciously or unconsciously, he had given to the malcontents. Louis XIII. was compelled to turn informer
against his quondam favourite, and to confess in a formal
document that he had encouraged Cinq-Mars in his
freedom of speech and action in order the better to
ascertain his real designs, and he asserted that the result
of this policy, more worthy of a spy than of a king, was
to convince him that his grand equerry was an enemy of
the state.

Armed with these depositions, Richelieu set out on
August 17 for Lyons by the Rhone, towing his prisoners

in another boat behind him. Bouillon had already been
sent to Lyons, and there the trial was held before twelve
commissioners, including the notorious and indispensable
Laubardemont. The guilt of Cinq-Mars was flagrant,
and he made no attempt to deny it; but the extent of
de Thou's complicity was by no means equally patent.
But any hesitation on the part of the judges was removed by the discovery of an ordinance of Louis XI.,
which declared that the concealment of a plot against
the state was an equal offence with actual partnership.
The two friends were both condemned to death on
September 12, and the sentence was carried out on the
same day. Their youth, their rigorous treatment, and
the heroism with which they met their fate, have earned
for Cinq-Mars and de Thou the sympathy both of contemporaries and posterity. This feeling was intensified
by the escape of Bouillon, who was at least equally
guilty; but he was the nephew of the prince of Orange,
an ally whom France had every reason to conciliate, and
he had a valuable hostage for his own life in the fortress
of Sedan. On condition that Sedan should be surrendered to the crown, Bouillon obtained a full pardon
for his numerous past offences.

The conspiracy of Cinq-Mars was the last episode of
importance in the life of Richelieu. The excitement of
the struggle had revived for a moment his failing powers,
but with its subsidence the process of decline became
more rapid than ever. Unable to leave his litter, he
was carried slowly from Lyons to Paris, travelling where-
ever possible by water. Everywhere he was received
with the respectful pomp usually displayed only for
royalty. In some towns the gates were too narrow to

admit the spacious litter, and the wall was promptly demolished to make room for its entry. At Fontainebleau the king came to meet him, and tried to atone for any past coldness by the unusual warmth of his greeting. From Paris Richelieu retired to his favourite residence at Rueil, where he received a visit from the queen, Anne of Austria, who seems to have at last been reconciled with her dying enemy. On November 4 he returned from Rueil to the Palais-Cardinal, which he was never to quit alive.

A sense of exultation may well have buoyed up the spirits of the dying statesman. He was master of France as he had never been before. His domestic enemies were utterly crushed. One of the most inveterate of his opponents, Mary de Medici, had died in this summer at Cologne, endeavouring to the last, by an intentional and exaggerated parade of poverty, to excite odium against the servant of old days whose ingratitude had reduced to such misery and degradation the mother of a French king and of the queens of Spain and England. From all quarters of Europe, from the Pyrenees, from Italy, from Franche Comté, from Germany, the news came of victories which convinced Richelieu that the work of his life was well done, and that the star of the Hapsburgs had paled before that of the Bourbons.

But this feeling of exultation, legitimate as it was, could not quicken his failing pulse, nor expel the fever from his weakened and emaciated frame. On November 29 the mischief spread to his lungs; he began to cough blood, and to experience great difficulty in breathing. Though he lingered for nearly a week, recovery was henceforth impossible. The doctors tried to relieve the fever by frequent bleedings, but the remedy only increased the general weakness. The king paid him two visits, and the cardinal took the opportunity to commend his relatives to the royal protection and favour, and to advise the choice of Mazarin as his own successor. The courage and composure with which he awaited an end which he knew to be inevitable excited the wonder and admiration of all his attendants. His intellect and his iron resolution were alike unaffected by the approach of death. Asked whether he pardoned his enemies, he replied: "Absolutely, and I pray God to condemn me, if I have had any other aim than the welfare of God and of the state."[1] On November 3, the regular physicians gave up all hope, and abandoned their patient to an empiric, whose prescriptions produced such a galvanic effect that the rumour of the cardinal's recovery spread through Paris. But the revival was only momentary; in the evening he relapsed into unconsciousness, which was only broken by occasional intervals till the following mid-day, when a groan and a last convulsion of the limbs announced that all was over, and that the man who had been for so many years the great motive-power in France had ceased to live.

Louis XIII.'s studied and habitual coldness of manner enabled him to avoid any display of feeling when the news arrived. "A great politician has departed!" was the only ejaculation that escaped him on hearing of the death of the minister whose greatness so completely

---

[1] This sentence, like the deathbed utterances of many other eminent men, has been corrupted by tradition into a more epigrammatic form. According to Madame de Motteville, Richelieu replied: "I have had no enemies except those of the state."

overshadowed and obscured his own character. But death did not free him immediately from the influence to which he had so long been accustomed to yield. The wishes of the deceased cardinal were carried out with scrupulous and almost ostentatious fidelity. Mazarin, who for the last year had shared all Richelieu's secrets, was admitted to the council of state the very day after his employer's death, and the other ministers were confirmed in their offices. The lesser posts which were vacated by Richelieu's death were divided among his relatives: the government of Brittany was conferred upon la Meilleraie; the offices of intendant of navigation and governor of Brouage were given to the marquis de Brézé; and the young Armand Jean de Pont-Courlay, who assumed his great-uncle's title of duc de Richelieu, received also the governorship of Havre. A royal circular to the provincial governors and parliaments, dated December 5, announced the king's determination "to maintain all the arrangements made during the ministry of the late cardinal, and to carry out all the plans concerted with him for the conduct of affairs both at home and abroad." A decree for the formal exclusion of the duke of Orleans from the regency, which had been drawn up in deference to Richelieu's wishes, was registered on December 9, in spite of the urgent entreaties of Gaston's daughter, the famous Mademoiselle. The numerous prisoners and exiles, who had hailed the news of the cardinal's death as the signal for their own release and triumph, discovered, to their disgust and disappointment, that no leniency was to be expected from the government.

But no man can continue long to rule from the

tomb, and the strenuous and resolute policy of Richelieu
was unsuited to the more subtle and agile mind of his
successor.   Mazarin had all an Italian's love for the
refinements of intrigue, and was confident that it was
both safer and easier to bend his opponents than to try
to break them.   Gradually a new policy of leniency
and concession was introduced instead of the older
methods of stern repression.   The prison doors were
opened, and the eager exiles were allowed to return to
France.   The decree against Gaston was revoked, and
he was even nominated to the office of lieutenant-governor
of the kingdom during the approaching minority.   The
change of attitude involved dangers and difficulties,
which Mazarin may have foreseen, and which he certainly succeeded in the end in overcoming.   But Louis
XIII., whose growing ill-health made him the passive
instrument of his new adviser, did not live to witness
the results of the change.   His death (May 14, 1643)
left his widow and infant son to face the problems of
domestic disorder and rebellion, and the consequent
prolongation of the war with Spain.   That the Fronde
proved in the end a harmless and almost a ridiculous
movement was due to Richelieu, who had deprived the
nobles and parliaments of all substantial power; that
the Fronde occurred at all was due to Mazarin's inability
to rule with the same iron hand as his more illustrious
predecessor.

It is needless to dilate further upon the greatness of
Richelieu's achievements, or upon the magnitude of the
influence which he exercised upon both France and
Europe.   That influence was so great and so lasting

that it continued to be felt until a new France and a
new Europe were evolved from the ruins caused by the
Revolution and by the insensate ambition of Napoleon,
and even then it was not wholly extinct. In the case
of France, indeed, it may be held that the traditions of
Richelieu's administration were regarded with excessive
and almost fatal veneration. In the next century, when
domestic conditions had become almost intolerable, and
when wholly new problems had arisen in foreign politics,
one generation of ministers after another adhered with
blind tenacity and fidelity to the old lines of French
policy. By these methods, and under these conditions,
France had been raised to greatness, and it was unconsciously argued that to depart from them must result
in bringing the country to ruin. Two instances out of
many may suffice to illustrate the excessive importance
attached to Richelieu's example. In order to check the
power of Austria in the east, Richelieu had organised a
policy of alliance with three client states—Sweden,
Poland, and Turkey. In the eighteenth century these
three states had so declined in power that they could
no longer serve the purpose for which France had
supported them, and in the meantime a wholly new
factor had been introduced into eastern politics by the
rise of Russia. A great statesman would have seen the
necessity of modifying the policy of France to suit these
altered conditions, but the French Government persisted
in regarding the maintenance of the client states as its
primary duty. The result was to alienate Russia and
to force her into an unnatural alliance with Austria, and
France had in consequence to suffer the profound humiliation of witnessing the partition of Poland without being

able to move a finger for its prevention. Again, the dominant aim of Richelieu's foreign policy was to abase the house of Hapsburg, and this end was achieved partly by himself and partly by his successors following in his footsteps. So thoroughly was the work done that in the next century the Hapsburgs had wholly ceased to be formidable to France, and French interests imperatively demanded the maintenance of Austria to secure the balance of power in Europe. But the permanence of the Richelieu tradition prevented France from grasping this patent fact until 1756, and till then the government continued to act as if its primary duty was to erase Austria from the list of great states. This led directly to the elevation of Prussia, destined to deal a terrible blow to French ascendency and prestige, and to the forfeiture to England of the leading part in maritime and colonial enterprise.

It only remains to say something of the character of the great statesman whose career has been sketched in the foregoing pages. It is impossible to contend that Richelieu was wholly admirable as a man, however much admiration may be extorted by his political achievements. His portrait in the Louvre, the master-piece of Philip of Champagne, impresses the observer with the conviction that he was no vulgar, domineering bully. His clear-cut and delicate features—the white hair contrasting sharply with the dark moustache and pointed beard—suggest rather the man of letters or the ascetic priest than the masterful politician who for so many years dominated both France and her enemies. But there is the suggestion at once of power and of irritability in the thin and compressed lips. One realises

that it is the face of a man who has suffered much,
even if he has achieved much; of a man who has not
gained his end without pain and labour. The fact that
Richelieu's health was never strong, and that he was
constantly subject to physical pain, must be always
borne in mind if we wish really to understand his
character and to appreciate the marvel of the work
which he accomplished. From his early manhood he
suffered from excruciating headaches—the result of a
fever contracted in the marshes of Poitou,—and these
often lasted for several days at a time. In one of his
letters he says: "I think I have one of the worst heads
in the world," and adds with a touch of humour not
usual with him, "There are many who will agree with
this, but in another sense."

In spite of this physical weakness his industry was
incessant and exhausting. He was not one of those
statesmen who are content to frame the broad lines of
policy and to leave the details to be worked out by
subordinates. Nothing was too small or unimportant
for his attention, though he never lost sight of the
general aim amid the multiplicity of minute details.
His system of spies was the most extensive and alert
that was ever organised by any statesman. And the
activity of his informants was by no means limited to
affairs of state; they had to bring the latest gossip
from the salons, the news of literary productions and
quarrels, the current talk of the streets and the theatres.
The cardinal's information was always so full and accurate
that it was believed that priests betrayed to him the
secrets of the confessional. On one occasion the papal
nuncio brought him, as a great piece of intelligence,

the overtures made by Gaston to the vice-legate of
Avignon. Richelieu acknowledged the communication
by stating the terms of the answer returned by the
vice-legate. But he had to pay the penalty for his
multifarious knowledge in the enormous amount of
labour which it entailed. Night and day secretaries
were in attendance to copy from his dictation or his
rough drafts. Many of his personal letters are dated
in the night. It was his habit to go to bed about
eleven, and after sleeping for four or five hours to rise
and work till six, when he would return to bed to
snatch another brief interval of oblivion till he rose for
the day ·between half-past seven and eight.

The whole weight of affairs rested upon Richelieu.
He was not only a first minister, but practically a sole
minister. The mistrust inspired by his numerous and
watchful enemies impelled him to keep all the strings
of home and foreign politics, of military and naval
administration, in his own hands; and the responsibility must have been at times almost overwhelming to
a man who lived a life so essentially solitary. Nothing
in Richelieu's career is more striking than his isolation.
He had dependents, flatterers, and tools in plenty;
but with the exception of the mysterious Father Joseph
he had no confidential friend, no one with whom he
could freely discuss personal and public affairs, no one
who could relieve him of some part of his burden by
sharing his secrets and anxieties. He was extremely in-
accessible; even foreign envoys could only gain admission
to his presence when the business to be discussed was of
special importance. He never quitted his residence without the attendance of his personal bodyguard, paid from

his own purse and officered by his own nominees. Even
in the royal palace he insisted upon retaining their
services. It was this habit of jealous suspicion, rather
than the prompting of family affection, that led him to
promote to high office his own relatives, as his brother-
in-law, de Brézé, his cousin, la Meilleraie, and his
nephew, de Pont-Courlay. His own colleagues in the
ministry were little more than clerks who carried out
instructions received from the cardinal.

The burden of labour and responsibility which devolved upon Richelieu, partly by his own choice and
partly by compulsion, must have been rendered all the
heavier by the extraordinary uncertainty of his own
position. The king's health was never strong, and on
several occasions his life was in serious danger from
disease. If he had died at any time before the birth
of the dauphin—born, it must be remembered, after
twenty-two years of barren wedlock—the royal power,
which Richelieu himself had so immensely strengthened,
would have passed at once to the cardinal's arch-enemy,
Gaston of Orleans. Nor was Richelieu's hold over
Louis XIII. by any means secure, at any rate in the
earlier years of his ministry. Louis was no mere puppet,
as has been often represented. His understanding was
retentive though slow ; he took a keen interest in
public business, especially in its details, and he had a
large share of the obstinacy and self-confidence of his
mother. In order to obtain and keep the king's
confidence, in spite of the domestic and other influences
always at work against him, Richelieu had to act with
great tact and caution. He never ventured to take
any step without the king's consent, and it is certain

that Louis would never have tolerated such an assertion of independent authority. Hence the necessity of constant conferences or correspondence, which the courtiers hoped and believed would so bore the king that he would ultimately seek to escape from such enthralling conditions. On every minute point of policy and administration Richelieu found it necessary not only to convince Louis—in itself a toilsome task—but also to create in his mind the impression that the ultimate decision was not the overmastering will of the minister but the independent product of the royal intellect. While Richelieu was so stern and awe-inspiring towards the outside world, he had to play the supple and pliant courtier in the presence of the master on whose favour and confidence all his own authority was based.

The charge most frequently brought against Richelieu is that of cruelty and vindictiveness, and it is a charge that cannot possibly be denied. Among the victims who perished on the scaffold for opposition to his rule were "five dukes, four counts, a marshal of France, and the king's favourite equerry, Cinq-Mars." To these must be added a number of lesser offenders who were put to death, and the many opponents, of all ranks, who were condemned to imprisonment in the Bastille or driven into exile in foreign lands by the minister whose enmity they had incurred. But if Richelieu was pitiless, he was not, like most revengeful despots, either capricious or unjust. He did not strike the tool if he could reach the employer; nor did he strike till guilt was obvious and incontestable; his was no reckless reign of terror. His methods, though often arbitrary and contrary to legal custom and tradition, were always fearless and above-board. Political considerations sometimes made it impossible to inflict a fitting penalty upon men who richly deserved it, such as de Bouillon and the traitorous Gaston, but the motive that allowed them to escape was never terror nor a wish to curry favour. And the experience of Mazarin's administration supplies a retrospective justification for Richelieu's severity. He was undoubtedly right from his own point of view in acting upon the maxim of Machiavelli that "it is safer to be feared than to be loved." It was the sense of impunity that had made the nobles independent and rebellious; this feeling had been strengthened by the concessions and pardons of the regency, and the only way to remove it and to compel obedience was by making their punishments prompt, severe, and impartial. The element of personal resentment, which seems to disfigure and condemn Richelieu's pitiless treatment of his foes, is accounted for by the sublime confidence with which he identified his own ascendency with the welfare of the state, a confidence without which few rulers have been able to achieve really great work. Finally, whatever we may think of the morality of Richelieu's actions, it is impossible not to be impressed by the magnificent courage with which, almost single-handed, he faced the most powerful nobles of the land, allied as they were with members of the royal family, and backed up from outside by great foreign powers. And this courage becomes the more memorable when we remember that Richelieu was no demagogue, supported by the enthusiastic and encouraging applause of the masses of the people. On the contrary, the successes which attended France were obscured to contemporaries by the material sufferings which were caused by military expenditure and defective financial wisdom. In his later years Richelieu was detested by the populace, and it is said that bonfires were kindled in many provinces of the kingdom to celebrate the death of the statesman who has been hailed by the almost unanimous opinion of later generations as the grandest figure among those who have contributed most to the greatness of France.

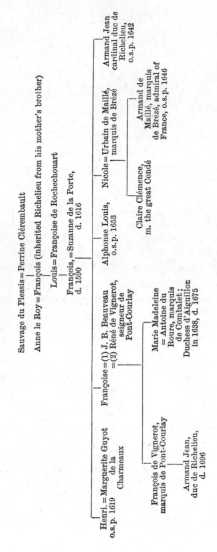

Sauvage du Plessis = Perrine Clérembault

Anne le Roy = François (inherited Richelieu from his mother's brother)

Louis = Françoise de Rochechouart

François, = Suzanne de la Porte, d. 1590, d. 1616

Henri, = Marguerite Guyot de la Charmeaux, o.s.p. 1619

Françoise = (1) J. B. Beauveau = (2) Réné de Vignerot, seigneur de Pont-Courlay

Alphonse Louis, o.s.p. 1653

Nicole = Urbain de Maillé, marquis de Brézé

Armand Jean cardinal duc de Richelieu, o.s.p. 1642

François de Vignerot, marquis de Pont-Courlay

Armand Jean, duc de Richelieu, d. 1696

Marie Madeleine = Antoine du Roure, marquis de Combalet; Duchess d'Aiguillon in 1638, d. 1675

Claire Clémence, m. the great Condé

Armand de Maillé, marquis of Brézé, admiral of France, o.s.p. 1646

APPENDIX B

THE CHIEF BOOKS ON THE PERIOD

I HAVE not attempted to compile a complete bibliography of writings on the age of Richelieu, nor even to draw up a list of all the authorities which I have consulted. My only object is to call the attention of the reader, who may wish to make a more detailed study of the period, to those books which he is likely to find most helpful and accessible.

Richelieu, *Mémoires*, 1610-1638 (Petitot's collection, 2nd series, xxi.-xxx. ; Michaud et Poujoulat, 2nd series, vii.-ix.).

Richelieu, *Succincte narration des grandes actions du Roi* (Petitot, 2nd series, xi. ; Michaud et Poujoulat, 2nd series, ix.).

Richelieu, *Lettres, Instructions Diplomatiques et Papiers d'État*, edited by M. d'Avenel. Paris, 8 volumes, 1853-1877.

Harangue pour la présentation des cahiers, ou clôture de l'assemblée, aux États, prononcé par l'évêque de Luçon, orateur du clergé (Petitot, 2nd series xi., p. 201).

Fontenay-Mareuil, *Mémoires* (Petitot, 1st series, l., li ; Michaud et Poujoulat, 2nd series, v.).

Bassompierre, *Mémoires* (Michaud et Poujoulat, 2nd series, vi.).

De Brienne, *Mémoires* (Michaud et Poujoulat, 3rd series, iii. ; Petitot, 2nd series, xxxv., xxxvi.).

D'Estrées, *Mémoires* (Michaud et Poujoulat, 2nd series, vi.).

De Pontis, *Mémoires* (Michaud et Poujoulat, 2nd series, vi.).

Mathieu Molé, *Mémoires* (Société de l'Histoire de France, Paris, 1855-1857).

Omer-Talon, *Mémoires* (Michaud et Poujoulat, 3rd series, vi.).

Arnauld d'Andilly, *Mémoires* (Michaud et Poujoulat, 2nd series, ix.).

Madame de Motteville, *Mémoires* (Michaud et Poujoulat, 2nd series, x.).

De Rohan, *Mémoires* (1610-1629) and *Mémoires sur la Guerre de la Valtelline* (Michaud et Poujoulat, 2nd series, v.).

Montchal, *Mémoires* (Rotterdam, 1718).

Aubéry, *L'Histoire du Cardinal-Duc de Richelieu* (Paris, 1660 ; Cologne, 2 volumes, 1666).

Aubéry, *Mémoires pour l'histoire du Cardinal-Duc de Richelieu* (Paris, 1660 ; Cologne, 5 volumes, 1667).

Martineau, *Le Cardinal de Richelieu*, tome i. (Paris, 1870).

Hanotaux, *Histoire du Cardinal de Richelieu*, tome i., *La jeunesse de Richelieu*, 1585-1614 (Paris, 1893).

Griffet, *Histoire du Règne de Louis XIII.* (Paris, 1758).

Bazin, *Histoire de France sous Louis XIII. et sous le ministère du Cardinal Mazarin* (4 volumes, Paris, 1846, 2nd edition).

Henri Martin, *Histoire de France*, tome xi. (4th edition, Paris, 1859).

Ranke, *Französische Geschichte, vornehmlich im sechszehnten und siebzehnten Jahrhundert*, Band ii. (Leipzig, 1876, Vierte Auflage).

D'Avenel, *Richelieu et la Monarchie Absolue* (4 volumes, Paris, 1884-1892).

Topin, *Louis XIII. et Richelieu, Étude Historique, accompagnée des lettres inédites du Roi au Cardinal de Richelieu* (2nd edition, Paris, 1876).

Caillet, *L'Administration en France sous le ministère du Cardinal de Richelieu* (Paris, 1857).

APPENDIX C

THE *TESTAMENT POLITIQUE*

ONE of the most keenly-debated points in connection with Richelieu is that of the authenticity of the *Testament Politique*, which was originally published at Amsterdam in 1688, and of which I have consulted the Paris edition of 1764. The first chapter, which has been printed in the collections of M. Petitot and of MM. Michaud and Poujoulat, under the title of *Succincte narration des grandes actions du Roi*, has been generally admitted to be a genuine work of the cardinal's, and to be equally authentic with the *Memoirs*. With this view I entirely agree. But the second chapter, the *Testament* proper, to which the *Succincte narration* serves as a sort of introduction, has been the subject of much discussion from the time of Voltaire downwards. In the present century there has been a growing tendency to treat it as an authoritative statement of Richelieu's political opinions in his later years. M. Henri Martin goes so far as to say that "the genius of the cardinal, whatever may be said to the contrary, is as obvious in the complete *Testament* as in the first chapter : the lion's mark is to be traced in a thousand passages, and the powerful personality of Richelieu is revealed by a crowd of traits which the abbè de Bourzeis could never have invented." This very positive opinion seems to me to be wholly untenable. The external evidence is quite indecisive one way or the other, but the internal evidence, both of style and matter, seems to be conclusive against the authenticity of the work. It is possible that the general plan may have been sketched out by Richelieu and filled in by a subordinate, but in that case it can hardly have undergone the cardinal's revision, and its value as evidence of his opinions is almost as slight as if it were an intentional forgery ; and the latter seems to me to be, on the whole, much the more probable solution. In accordance with this conviction I have carefully abstained —in spite of obvious temptations to the contrary—from making any use of the *Testament* as a guide to the real aims of Richelieu's policy. And I am further of opinion that, if its authenticity could be conclusively proved, the current estimates of Richelieu would have to be not merely added to, but profoundly modified. Especially the striking saying of Mignet, that " he intended everything which he achieved," would have to be abandoned, and many results of his rule, which are now attributed to intelligent purpose, would have to be regarded as the product of chance.

THE END

944.03Z
R528L

43814